Black Literate Lives

Black Literate Lives offers an innovative approach to understanding the complex and multi-dimensional perspectives of Black literate lives in the United States. Author Maisha T. Fisher reinterprets historiographies of Black self-determination and self-reliance to powerfully interrupt stereotypes of African American literacy practices. The book expands the standard definitions of literacy practices to demonstrate the ways in which minority groups keep their cultures and practices alive in the face of oppression, both inside and outside of schools.

This important addition to critical literacy studies:

- Demonstrates the relationship of an expanded definition of literacy to self-determination and empowerment
- Exposes unexpected sources of Black literate traditions of popular culture and memory
- Reveals how spoken word poetry, open mic events, and everyday cultural performances are vital to an understanding of Black literacy in the 21st century.

By centering the voices of students, activists, and community members whose creative labors past and present continue the long tradition of creating cultural forms that restore collective identity, *Black Literate Lives* ultimately uncovers memory while illuminating the literate and literary contributions of Black people in America.

Maisha T. Fisher is Assistant Professor in Language, Literacy, and Culture in the Division of Educational Studies at Emory University.

2009

JAN

EL

The Critical Social Thought Series

Edited by Michael W. Apple,
University of Wisconsin-Madison

Black Literate Lives

Historical and Contemporary Perspectives

Maisha T. Fisher

Routledge
Taylor & Francis Group

NEW YORK AND LONDON

First published 2009
by Routledge
270 Madison Ave, New York, NY 10016

Simultaneously published in the UK
by Routledge
2 Park Square, Milton Park, Abingdon, Oxon OX14 4RN

Routledge is an imprint of the Taylor & Francis Group, an informa business

© 2009 Taylor & Francis

Typeset in Minion by
Keystroke, 28 High Street, Tettenhall, Wolverhampton
Printed and bound in the United States of America on acid-free paper by
Edwards Brothers, Inc.

Library of Congress Cataloging-in-Publication Data
Fisher, Maisha T.
Black literate lives : historical and contemporary perspectives / Maisha T. Fisher.
    p. cm. — (The critical social thought series)
Includes bibliographical references (p.) and index.
1. American literature—African American authors—History and criticism—Theory, etc.
2. African Americans in literature. 3. African Americans—Intellectual life. I. Title.
PS153.N5F53 2008
810.9′896073—dc22   2008014942

ISBN 10: 0–415–95864–4 (hbk)
ISBN 10: 0–415–95865–2 (pbk)
ISBN 10: 0–203–89045–0 (ebk)

ISBN 13: 978–0–415–95864–6 (hbk)
ISBN 13: 978–0–415–95865–3 (pbk)
ISBN 13: 978–0–203–89045–5 (ebk)

For my brother, Damany, M. Fisher:
My son, hear the instruction of thy father, and forsake not the law of thy mother: For they shall be an ornament of grace unto thy head and chains about thy neck. (Proverbs 1: 8–9)

For Mom and Dad:
Deeds, not words.

Contents

Series Editor Introduction

I went to school and spent most of my formative years in Paterson, New Jersey. Paterson was one of the earliest industrial cities in the nation as well as one of the most radical cities politically. But it was also the home of many poets, writers, and artists. Indeed, art by and for the people was part of class and race mobilizations for decades in Paterson and many other parts of New Jersey. The fact that I was given the middle name of *Whitman*, the profane poet of the body and a New Jersey product himself, speaks to the power of the imagination and of people's art in the multi-racial poor and working-class community in which I was raised.

I say all of this at the beginning of my Series Editor's Introduction to *Black Literate Lives* in part because my own background makes me even more excited about what Maisha Fisher has accomplished in this book. It rings true to me. It brings back memories of struggles over representation, over how exploited and marginalized people could find ways of being heard. But it is not only personal memories that make this book significant. Fisher challenges us to rethink what we mean by literacy. She provides us with examples of literacy practices that go well beyond what many educators and others may be used to. And she connects these practices to a long history of struggles over what it means to build a vibrant "common" culture among subaltern groups.

Neoliberals and neoconservatives have not been shy about attacking the visions of literacy and culture that have been built by subaltern movements through decades of hard and creative work (Apple 2006; Buras 2008). They have sought to undermine the institutions that have advanced these claims to cultural legitimacy and authority and also to undermine the voices from below that advocate them. This of course is not new. But it is especially significant now, when such programs as No Child Left Behind and the constant attacks on public institutions put so many of the gains that have been made under threat.

We should not be surprised at this. Literacy has never been a neutral technical project. What counts as literacy, who should or should not have "it," what role it should perform, how it should be taught—all of this and more were the results of ongoing struggles between dominant and subaltern groups. These struggles have a very long history. And they are international as well as national.

Let me give two examples. Take the case of Voltaire, the leader of the Enlightenment who so wanted to become a member of the nobility. For him, the Enlightenment should begin with the "grands." Only when it had captured the hearts and minds of the commanding heights could it concern itself with the masses below. But for Voltaire and many of his followers, one caution should be taken very seriously. One should take every care to prevent the masses from learning to read (Apple 2000).

Voltaire is talking largely in class terms, although we also know that behind the Enlightenment was another vision of who could and could not be enlightened. The "racial other" stood out as the mirror against which the Enlightenment saw itself . Charles Mills powerfully states it this way: "One could say that the nonwhite body is a moving bubble of wilderness in white political space" (Mills 1997, p. 53).

This is made clear historically in the many murderous prohibitions against teaching slaves of African descent to read in the United States and the Caribbean. Thus, for example, in slave-holding Jamaica, the idea of literate "slaves" was dangerous and offensive to most whites. It could contaminate and erode "the exclusivity and sacrosanctity of European privilege and identity." Furthermore, it could illuminate "the murky underside of European 'civilization' and fantasy." Just as crucially, "it potentially threatened the physical security of the whites and their property by inciting slaves to visions of total freedom." Black people who went to great lengths to become literate—in the usual meaning of that term then—"might have pretensions of being something other than . . .

[white people's] economic tools" (Green 2007, pp. 177–178). Few things could be more threatening than the changed identities that undoubtedly would have arisen from this. Movements among enslaved people, Black actors going even further than their already constant daily organized and individual struggles in nearly every aspect of their lives—this was to be feared at all costs. And literacy in all of its forms among oppressed people was to be feared even more than the worries that Voltaire had.

This constant struggle over literacy—in *all* of its forms—is where *Black Literate Lives* enters and where it makes such a powerful contribution. It intervenes at multiple levels and multiple sites, from the realities and venues of popular culture to the lives and labor of teachers in more formal but still counter-hegemonic educational institutions.

We know that no liberatory movement can hope to succeed without creating the ground for thinking differently. Such a ground is a vital basis. It provides spaces for the construction both of one's own meanings and of new forms of solidarity and social relations (Fiske 1989, p. 10). Such meanings and relations are both a response to oppressive realities and help generate and shape these responses. But where are these grounds often found? C. L. R. James and others were not incorrect when they noted that popular cultural forms and content often bear the mark of genius of the oppressed (Buhle 1988, p. 101; see also McCarthy 1998). That genius is part of the story Fisher wishes to tell as she uncovers how common struggles to build and keep alive aesthetic and insurgent meanings are so much a part of a people's past and present.

This is an important point. A common culture involves full participatory meaning making. That is, a common culture isn't just "there." It is part of a collective process, one in which what counts as legitimate voices and traditions are constantly being remade and redefined. It is, thus, inseparable from ongoing struggle and radical transformation. As Eagleton puts it, such a notion "requires an ethic of common responsibility, full democratic participation at all levels of social life, including material production, and egalitarian access to the culture-fashioning process" (Eagleton 2000, p. 119).

The truly vital (in both senses of that word—crucial and alive with possibilities) nature of the aesthetic and meaning-making practices that Maisha Fisher so powerfully illuminates here is not only visible in the United States. These issues are clearly international and are gaining widespread attention. Stuart Hall, for example, has continued his decades-long labor to open up the public domain to voices and an aesthetic from below through the "inIVA" in Britain. While focusing largely on the visual arts and on issues of visual literacy, his efforts speak to the ways in which the continuing struggles over what counts as literacy and over whose voices are heard can open up spaces for subaltern voices and movements (Tawadros 2007, p. 64).

Like Stuart Hall and many others, in *Black Literate Lives*, Maisha Fisher demonstrates how the creative impulses found within multiple literacy practices enable new possibilities and new forms of cultural and political solidarity to emerge. That by itself would be enough to make this an extremely valuable volume. But Fisher goes further. By bringing all of this to light, she also points to new possibilities from which all committed educators throughout the world have much to learn.

Michael W. Apple
John Bascom Professor of Curriculum and Instruction
and Educational Policy Studies
University of Wisconsin–Madison

Foreword

The Preface to Henry Louis Gates' edited volume, *"Race," Writing, and Difference* (1986) provides a salient lens through which to ground the interpretation of literacy and empowerment that forms the foundation of Maisha Fisher's argument in this present text. Gates introduces the essays in this volume with an exposé of the ways in which Enlightenment thinkers, consistently credited for their influence on the minds of men who would form the foundations of republicanism in America, also generated the discourse that would lead to a belief that African Americans were thwarted in the advance toward civilization and, thus, occupied "a lower place in the great chain of being." The conclusion that those of a darker hue were lesser versions of humanity rested distinctly on the central act of literacy itself: writing. For Enlightenment thinkers, writing was the premier symbol of reason. Indeed, distinct from other fine arts, Gates posits that for Enlightenment gurus, writing was "the visible sign of reason itself" since writing was "the medium of reason's expression." If Africans, thus, did not record their history in writing, their failure could be equated, as far as the Europeans were concerned, with the failure of African Americans to achieve humanity. In other words, "without writing, no respectable sign of the workings of reason, of mind, could exist."

The response of African Americans from the early national period through the antebellum era to the proscribed limitations of their personhood because of a lack of knowledge of European norms of writing has been captured in varied historical descriptions, each detailing the efforts of a people to become literate despite the limited opportunity and (often) prevailing hostility toward their efforts to do so. However, every case of literacy on the part of enslaved Africans challenged Enlightenment ideas about African American deficiency and some compelling cases actually demanded an affidavit from other Whites since the capacity to reason in a written form violated the expectation of African American failure. The life story of George Moses Horton provides one example. In the Foreword to his book, *Naked Genius* (1982), the slave George Moses Horton is described as memorizing his verses in his head when he could not yet even write. Indeed, he claimed to have "composed at the handle of a plow" the lines that White University of North Carolina students, incredulous at his poetic abilities, voraciously translated into writing as he recited his creations. Horton would later become proficient at writing and publish three books. Yet, the Foreword to his efforts would have to be validated by reputable Whites who could affirm that the writings were indeed those of a southern Black slave, previously illiterate. Likewise, Phillis Wheatley, the first African American poet, would need the affirmations of Whites that her poetry was authentic (Gates, 1986). For enslaved African Americans to become the conduits through which reasoned language could emerge in written form challenged the White supremacy that formed the very foundations upon which the country was being built.

The collective synergy of African American literary endeavors from slavery to the "freedom" generated by the Civil War has been captured eloquently and persuasively in Dickson D. Bruce's *The Origins of African American Literature* (2001). The text exemplifies the ways in which, as Gates terms it, African Americans used literacy to write their way to freedom. Deeply situated in the historical complexities of the period, Bruce captures the centrality of slave narratives, newspapers, and other literacy endeavors, demonstrating the necessity of African Americans' use of literacy as the means to freedom. In the descriptions provided, literacy cannot be reduced to merely acquiring the skills to read and write; rather, it manifests itself as a powerful, political form of voice where the mechanics of reading and writing are emboldened with purpose. His book, however, despite the compelling accounts it offers, ends its chronology in 1865.

For a continuation of his insightful analysis into another historical moment, we have Maisha Fisher to thank. Fisher's insightful chronology both follows Bruce's intellectual tradition and extends its parameters. Had the White South shifted its views of African Americans after the powerful narratives and poetry African Americans wrote during the antebellum period, the tradition of powerful literacy Fisher unveils in a later era might have been mitigated. However, the South was resistant to accepting new perspectives on African Americans after Reconstruction, preferring to cling instead to long-held values about the place of the darker brother in the economy of the republic for another 100 years. With this perspective still entrenched, Winthrop D. Jordan's assertions about Europeans' pre-1700 attitudes about Negroes, not unexpectedly, resonate sharply with the postulations about Blacks that resounded in the post-Brown resistance to school desegregation (Jordan, 1968; Kilpatrick, 1962). As John Hope Franklin captured the dilemma in *Racial Equality in America*: "David Walker, in his *Appeal* of 1829, sought to perform the task for his progeny by striking a blow for equality. But Martin Luther King had to do it all over again as though David Walker had never lived" (Franklin, 1976, p. 73). Franklin's assertion captures the extent to which the need for a powerful literacy from Reconstruction to the Civil Rights movement was as central an ingredient for freedom as had been the literacy movements of the previous era.

Brilliantly conceived, Fisher's text provides the lens through which to view this latter period. Focusing primarily on the civil rights era and continuing into the present, Fisher compels an expanded view of literacy of African Americans which has often been reduced during this period to discussions of access to school and to performance on standardized tests. While schools provide an important mechanism through which literacy can be acquired, the chronologies of the school experiences of Black children during this period seldom illuminate the ways in which African Americans continued to use literacy in powerful ways to propel themselves toward freedom. In Fisher's description, however, as in previous eras, newspapers and poems again become the foundation of an African American community seeking its liberation. In so doing, Fisher skillfully renders visible the connections between literacy and Black empowerment that are sometimes masked in traditional histories of schools.

Her insightful text links the agency of African American parents from New York to California with the long history of antebellum efforts to promote a powerful literacy. As a result, the work captures a new bend in the long journey toward freedom in a country that has consistently belittled the efforts of African Americans to participate as freed men. Consistent with her own previous book on literacy in out-of-school places and with Elizabeth McHenry's *Forgotten Readers*, Fisher demonstrates the ways in which literacy forms of a previous era continued to be the tools through which African Americans sought freedom and equality. Even today, as Fisher eloquently demonstrates, African Americans continue to seek to use a powerful literacy to make Thomas Jefferson's postulations about Enlightenment freedoms their own.

The challenge Fisher's book forces contemporary literacy educators to address is captured in her personal memoirs about the activities of her own parents, outlined in the book's "Introduction." In seeking to train a daughter to understand the importance of, and the power of, the Black literate voice, Fisher's parents' activities easily become the contemporary exemplars depicting the continuance of the tradition upon which her book is grounded. For their little girl, divorcing power from literacy was not an option, hence their efforts to provide a powerful literacy in initiating their own school and in their efforts to seek a Black teacher who would "other parent" the literacy forms they sought in the integrated setting where she was schooled. Their behaviors, the behaviors of their predecessors, and the behaviors of their contemporaries, as Fisher describes them here, indict the prevailing national trend to ensure that no African American child is left behind in acquiring the mechanical skills of reading and writing while divorcing the children of African descent from a heritage of powerful literacy. Fisher's book poignantly challenges the error of this practice.

If African Americans are to address the inequalities that still plague their experiences, the heritage of powerful literacy must be reclaimed in the education of African American children. For children who can no longer identify Frederick Douglass, or W. E. B. DuBois either as people or as experts in the use of language—and these children exist—reconnecting mechanical forms of literacy with powerful forms of literacy must be a central component of their education since, unfortunately, the truth remains that African Americans are still on the journey to write a way to freedom. Fisher brilliantly uses this book to connect the familiar well-trod path of liberation for African American people with the new, uncharted and sometimes unknown demonstrations of powerful literacy in this sphere and time. It challenges a people to understand the trap of enslavement of mind and body, and it commands readers to recognize the manner in which powerful literacy can still free a people. Moreover, the work challenges literacy educators and others to be certain that the forms of literacy she describes are not lost to a new generation of teacher educators and concerned parents. Fisher's book is central, foundational reading for all those who would aspire to educate African American children.

Vanessa Siddle Walker
Professor, Educational Studies
Emory University

References

Apple, M. W. (2000). *Official knowledge: Democratic education in a conservative age* (2nd ed.). New York: Routledge.

—— (2006). *Educating the "right" way: Markets, standards, God, and inequality* (2nd ed.). New York: Routledge.

Apple, M. W., & Buras, K. L. (Eds.). (2006). *The subaltern speak: Curriculum, power, and educational struggles.* New York: Routledge.

Bruce, Jr., D. D. (2001). *The origins of African American literature, 1680–1865.* Charlottesville, VA: University Press of Virginia.

Buhle, P. (1988). *C. L. R. James: The artist as revolutionary.* New York: Verso.

Buras, K. L. (2008). *Rightist multiculturalism: Core lessons on neoconservative school reform.* New York: Routledge.

Eagleton, T. (2000). *The idea of culture.* Oxford: Blackwell.

Fiske, J. (1989). *Reading the popular.* Boston: Unwin Hyman.

Franklin, J. H. (1976). *Racial equality in America.* Chicago: University of Chicago Press.

Gates, H. L. (1986). *"Race," writing, and difference.* Chicago: University of Chicago Press.

Green, C. (2007). Unspeakable worlds and muffled voices. In B. Meeks (Ed.) *Culture, politics, race, and diaspora: The thought of Stuart Hall* (pp. 151–184). London: Lawrence and Wishart.

Horton, G. M. (1982). *Naked genius.* Greensboro: Greensboro Printing Company [Chapel Hill Historical Society].

Jordan, W. D. (1968). *White over Black: American attitudes toward the Negro, 1550–1812.* Chapel Hill, NC: University of North Carolina Press.

Kilpatrick, J. J. (1962). *The southern case for school segregation.* New York: Crowell-Collier Publishing Company.

McCarthy, C. (1998). *The uses of culture.* New York: Routledge.

McHenry, E. (2002). *Forgotten readers: Recovering the lost history of African American literary societies.* Durham, NC: Duke University Press.

Mills, C. (1997). *The racial contract.* Ithaca, NY: Cornell University Press.

Tawadros, G. (2007). The revolution stripped bare. In B. Meeks (Ed.), *Culture, politics, race, and diaspora: The thought of Stuart Hall* (pp. 64–72). London: Lawrence and Wishart.

Acknowledgments

Michael Apple was instrumental in making this project happen. I am grateful to Michael for his vision and for giving me tremendous encouragement to tell this story for the Critical Social Thought Series.

I would like to thank the organizers and participants in the spoken word poetry venues and Black bookstore events who invited me to be a part of their lives during my dissertation research at the University of California, Berkeley: The McNeal Family and Straight Out Scribes at Carol's Books in Sacramento, California; Khiry Malik, Supercaliflow-linguistics, and the Mahogany Crew in Sacramento, California; Greg Bridges and the Jahva House Speak Easy family in Oakland, California; and the Richardson family at Marcus Books in Oakland and San Francisco, California. More specifically, I want to express my profound respect and admiration for all the poets and writers who have allowed me to reprint their poetry and music over the years: Negesti, Scorpio Blues, NerCity, and Gabrilla Ballard.

Cathie Wright-Lewis, or Mama Cathie, my dear friend and colleague, helped make parts of this project possible the day she invited me to her spoken word poetry circle at Benjamin Banneker Academy for Community Development in Brooklyn, New York. She is a tireless educator and advocate for our young people.

Ayanna McNeil, my student, my teacher, and little sister, has been a supportive force throughout this process. It has been a joy and honor to watch this young woman evolve and continue to craft her poetry and prose.

I am deeply indebted to Baba Jitu Weusi (a.k.a. Les Campbell and formerly known as "Big Black") who accepted a phone call from a stranger (me) after living through the era of the strategic infiltration of Independent Black Institutions and COINTELPRO. Baba Weusi helped me make sense of the collection of *Black News* newspapers that I inherited from my parents and provided the back story of the emergence of this publication. I am grateful for establishments such as The Schomburg Center for Research in Black Culture in Harlem, New York City, and The Night of the Cookers Café in Fort Greene, Brooklyn, who allowed Baba Weusi and me to sit and talk as long as we needed. Baba Weusi also introduced me to two amazing black-owned and operated bookstores, A&B Books and Dare Books in Brooklyn, New York City, where we spent a great deal of time browsing, talking, and buying. I also appreciate Studio 281 in Atlanta, Georgia, and the hospitality of Henri Davenporte in particular, which served as an ideal place to introduce Baba Weusi and his lovely wife, Angela, to Atlanta's jazz community.

Professor Kwasi Konadu, scholar and former director of the Council of Independent Black Institutions (CIBI), trusted me with Jitu Weusi's address and phone number so that I could request an interview for this book. It's good to know that the "Underground Railroad" is still running.

Kristen Buras, my dear colleague, walked in the doors of the Division of Educational Studies at Emory University and encouraged me to complete this research project and begin this book manuscript. I am deeply indebted to Kristen for reading one of the first drafts of the manuscript and giving me critical and specific feedback.

Vanessa Siddle Walker graciously read an earlier draft of the manuscript. Her wisdom and insight are cherished and valued. Vanessa has been instrumental in helping me articulate links between history and literacy.

Sarah Warshauer Freedman saw this research in the seedling form. Although I did not pursue this as my topic for my dissertation, Sarah was incredibly supportive when I explored it tangentially to my research. I appreciate her commitment to seeing me through this project.

Additionally, I have many colleagues who have engaged me as I have thought about this work over the years: H. Samy Alim, Arnetha Ball, Jennifer Gandhi, Marc Hill, Jackie Jordan Irvine, Valerie Kinloch, David

Kirkland, Carol D. Lee, Geneva Smitherman (Dr. G.), Caroline Streeter, and Erica Walker.

Students in my class, "History of African American Literacies" (a.k.a. "The Valentine Readers Society"), deserve special recognition for being patient with my enthusiasm (okay–more like fanaticism) during this course that served as a foundation for the book project. Roxanne Comegys, Keisha Green, Carey Smith-Marchi, Andrea Hefflin, Ellington Lang, Megan Callier, and Hamzat Sani helped me take the class beyond the corridors of the North Decatur building and into the community including the Shrine of the Black Madonna Bookstore and Cultural Center and the Nsoromma School.

Catherine Bernard and Heather Jarrow at Routledge made the ride smooth. I appreciate their enthusiasm, support, and most of all their patience!

Dr. James and Cheryl Fisher, my parents, and my brother, Damany M. Fisher had everything to do with this book. This is our story. Coming of age, I always knew that our lives, and thus Black lives, were more than the mediocrity and mayhem that are often depicted in the media. This book is dedicated to every FREE community event we converged upon, every lecture we attended, certainly every jazz concert, and cultural arts festival we gathered at as a family and every newspaper, pamphlet, program and book we picked up along the way. I especially appreciate the thoughtful comments my father offered about the manuscript and for reintroducing me to the humility of red ink. Lastly, I appreciate my father's movement to help me leave my "comfort words" (something like "comfort foods") behind. If there are any left in this book—it is "*my bad*."

I will always be appreciative of my extended family and the many ways in which they instilled the love of words and language both written and spoken in me. I especially wish to acknowledge my cousin/brother, Narryn Fisher, who consistently challenges me intellectually and creatively (yes, we know why the caged bird beatboxes). I am humbled that he makes time to read my work in spite of the fact he is doing the real work on the ground with his beautiful sons Kemit, Kareem, and Kamal. Let the circle be unbroken.

I'd like to acknowledge Sage Publications (*Written Communication*), the National Council of Teachers of English and specifically (*Research in the Teaching of English*) the National Society for the Study of Education (NSSE), for granting me permission to reprint parts of my previously published articles for Chapter 1, Chapter 4, and Chapter 5 respectively.

Nichole Shields of Brooks Permissions helped me navigate the permissions terrain with a great deal of graciousness and generosity. In addition to helping me obtain the permission to use Gwendolyn Brooks's poems, "The Blackstone Rangers," "Young Afrikans," and "Speech to the Young/Speech To the Progress Toward," she also took interest in my work and sent kind words along the way.

I am grateful to Bob Crawford for granting me permission to use his brilliant photo, "Gwendolyn Brooks at the Wall of Respect" taken in Chicago, Illinois. I would also like to thank Professor Margo Crawford, his daughter, for helping facilitate the process.

Lastly, I wish to acknowledge Emory University, and specifically the Emory College Office, the Dean's Office for their assistance with permissions.

An Introduction

Not Yet Free

As a child I remember playing with seven life-size blocks made from recycled cardboard boxes. My father had carefully wrapped the boxes with white butcher paper and spray-painted them red to give the impression of bricks. I, however, thought they looked more like gifts. The front of each block had words painted in capitalized bold, black letters: UMOJA, KUJICHAGULIA, UJIMA, UJAMAA, NIA, KUUMBA, and IMANI. These "building" blocks were a part of my everyday existence; some days I would stack them high or lay them side by side in the living room. From time to time I would take some of the blocks outside where they might get left overnight among outdoor toys, nestled in a patch of ivy or blocking one of the many dirt paths my parents excavated in our backyard. In theory, I had memorized these seven words, known as the Nguzo Saba, and I also learned to light a candle for each principle during a celebration called Kwanzaa which began the day after Christmas and lasted through New Year's Day. My family, like many Black families seeking an alternative to the commercialization of Christmas in the 1970s, internalized the abbreviated translations of the Nguzo Saba: Unity, Self-Determination, Collective Work and Responsibility, Cooperative Economics, Purpose, Creativity, and Faith. Maulana Karenga, the creator of Kwanzaa, studied Kiswahili and used this pan-African language as a foundation for "countering the denigration of African culture endemic to American racial discourse" (Brown, 2003, p. 16).[1]

The Nguzo Saba was also part of the foundation of a Black community school co-founded by my mother, Cheryl Fisher. Named Shule Jumamose, or Saturday School, the school was located in Sacramento's mostly Black Oak Park neighborhood in a large craftsmen style house originally constructed for a prominent physician. The building was eventually acquired by my parents (Simpson, 2004). Shule Jumamose emerged from a conference called "Gettin' It Together! A Service Conference for Black Survival" organized by The Sacramento Black Awareness Committee on Saturday, May 8, 1971, at Sacramento State University. My parents were among a movement of concerned Black parents, educators, and students across the United States who saw a dire need to either supplement or provide an alternative to the public school education for Black youth. My mother, Cheryl Fisher, explained the purpose for a school like Shule Jumamose to a local news reporter:

> We started Shule Jumamose because as parents and as black people we are concerned about the education black children are getting in public schools. Because it in no way reinforces their well-being nor does it create a sense of pride.
>
> ("New school aims to aid Black youth,"
> *The Sacramento Bee*, Wednesday, June 23, 1971, p. B3)

Shule Jumamose ("Saturday School") was an Independent Black Institution (IBI) that not only taught the traditional content areas found in American public schools but also encouraged its students to be literate in African Diasporic, geography, cultures, literature, and music. In December 1970, the school hosted Sacramento's first Black Film Festival with a range of topics including Les Ballet Africaines, Blues music, Marcus Garvey and the Black Panther Party. The film festival included oral narrations by my father and other scholars ("Black Film Festival," *Sacramento Observer*, December 1970). Shule was also the first institution in Sacramento to host a Kwanzaa celebration; for organizers of independent Black educational institutions, "promoting Kwanzaa was an extension of building an independent school, a community center, or participating in Third World political struggles" (Mayes, 2006, p. 242).[2] The pedagogy of Shule Jumamose was informed by the Black Arts and Black Power Movements that fused together poetry, prose, music, theater written for, by, and about Black people throughout the African Diaspora using oral, aural, and written strategies as a continuum. These movements of the late 1960s and the 1970s, and consequently Black institutions that were developed during this period vigorously fused literate practices with social protest. The efforts of my parents at Shule Jumamose were linked to a larger phenomenon of blending literate traditions with activism.

The aim of this book then is to examine how people of African descent have employed literate practices to create and sustain independent institutions in the United States and abroad that focus on the production and preservation of written and spoken words while generating a discourse of self-reliance among Black people. Self-reliance in this context is inextricably linked to Black people's struggle during their enslavement in the United States and their continued efforts to pursue freedom, literacy, education, and economic independence. Furthermore, this study seeks to understand how institution-building encouraged poets and writers to become educators, activists, community organizers, and leaders. Ideas, practices and values associated with literacy in these independent institutions often go unrecognized and undervalued in schools and formal institutions of teaching and learning (Fisher, 2003a, 2003b, 2004, 2006a, 2006b, 2007b). In her study of "forgotten readers," McHenry (2002) posits that people of African descent have historically had to organize their own literate and literary institutions due to denied access to and/or substandard educational opportunities. McHenry further argues that it is possible that scholarship examining literacy learning in African American communities may want to consider the "unexpected sources."

Extending this line of inquiry, I have examined the "unexpected sources" of Black literate traditions in the twenty-first century in out-of-school and school settings, such sources include spoken word poetry open mic venues often held in restaurants and cafés, Black-owned and operated bookstore events that have persevered in spite of the internet and bookstore chains as well as classrooms that use an open mic format to give students opportunities to share their original compositions (Fisher, 2004, 2005a, 2005b, 2007a). Using "ethnohistory" (Heath, 1981) and "historical ethnography" (Siddle Walker, 1996) methods, *Black Literate Lives* draws from both historical and ethnographic research methods including documentary source materials, oral histories and participant observation in what I refer to as Participatory Literacy Communities (PLCs) or literary societies, writers collectives, Black Community Schools, Black-owned and operated bookstores and poetry "houses" (see Appendix A for "Notes on Methodology"). *Black Literate Lives* is guided by the following questions:

- What are some of the historical perspectives of Black literate lives and specifically the values regarding the teaching and learning of literacy during the enslavement of African Americans and during Reconstruction?
- How have Black poets and writers redefined what it meant to be literate and literary in the 1960s? How does the life and writing of Gwendolyn Brooks demonstrate the shifting role of Black poets and writers from artists to literacy activists?
- What role(s) did Independent Black Institutions (IBIs), and specifically the EAST organization out of Brooklyn, New York, assume in the development of Black literate identities in the 1960s and 1970s? How did *Black News*, a newspaper published by the EAST, seek to redefine literacy to include community, arts, nutrition and overall well-being?
- In what ways have more recent institutions such as bookstores and cafés continued the literate traditions of Black poets, writers, and Independent Black Institutions of the 1960s and 1970s?
- How have Black teachers used the pedagogical strategies of literacy activism identified with Independent Black Institutions to advance literacy in urban high schools in the twenty-first century?

Independent Black Institutions like Shule Jumamose embodied the marriage between art, politics, education, and literacy seen in these movements. As a young adult, and prior to beginning my career as an educator, I would ask my father why he and my mother made such an investment in a school like Shule Jumamose. Not only did they invest time while holding full-time jobs, they also paid the mortgages for their home and for Shule's home. My parents sent my brother and me to integrated public schools kindergarten through twelfth grades in the Sacramento City Unified School District where they were fully engaged in school activities, flipped pancakes at school fundraisers, sat in uncomfortable chairs for Parent Teacher Association meetings, and generally made their presence known. My brother and I were also carefully placed in the hands of two African American teachers, Mrs.

Shelby in elementary school and Mr. Withrow in high school. Once again, it was through the organizing of these two teachers that orality, writing and social protest were interwoven. Participating in one of Mrs. Shelby's Black History Month programs in elementary school was not optional and Mr. Withrow encouraged us to participate in the Black Student Union (B.S.U) activities at our high school. B.S.U activities almost always involved the recitation of poems and speeches by African Americans for events throughout Northern California. We were messengers of sorts—sharing Black history and culture with our peers. While both teachers were products of segregated schools, Mrs. Shelby and Mr. Withrow served as lanterns and guides to Black students navigating their way through integrated schools. Shule Jumamose was closed before I reached school age and before my brother was born; however, the ethos of the school persevered and the values seemed to be omnipresent. And while Shule Jumamose no longer exists as a formal institution, its influence is carried by those who taught there and attended the programs and events. Throughout this book, I challenge readers to rethink fixed notions of institutions and consider them as ideologies, values, and beliefs that can exist without a formal building— an idea I return to in Chapter 1. Whenever my father responded to my question about why Shule Jumamose existed, he would repeat the mantra that was popular during the Black Power and Black Arts Movements, "Not yet uhuru," or "Not yet free." This phrase, a mix of English and Kiswahili made popular by Oginga Odinga's (1969) autobiography bearing the same title, embodied the traditions of these movements by liberating words through lived experience. Even as an assistant professor in history at a university, a position my father would later leave by choice, he believed Black people were still seeking mental, physical, spiritual, and most importantly educational liberation. In fact, the work of eradicating the discourse of self-hatred with cries of "Black is beautiful" for Black youth may be one of the most important gifts these movements and thus their institutions provided: "No other African American cultural movement has revolved so entirely around the purging, from the African American psyche of racial self-hatred, the internalization of anti-black ways of seeing and thinking" (Collins and Crawford, 2006, p. 10).

After some time, the red "building blocks" faded and the overall condition of these literacy artifacts deteriorated. I learned that the literacy artifacts that I thought were my toys were in fact the building blocks of Black cultural nationalism—a term I would not hear or begin to understand until well into my adulthood. My parents never identified themselves as Black Nationalists but took pride in being a hybrid family absorbing the practices that worked in their context. What I did know, however, was that my brother and I grew up surrounded by words, language, art, and politics. The many events we attended with our parents always included scholars, poets, authors, speakers, musicians, and artists seamlessly coming together to express themselves with a message or a political edge. These events would always have a wealth of reading material available (my parents always loaded us up with random papers from various organizations and institutions). If something was read, it was followed by speaking. If something was spoken, it was supported by reading. I always thought these elements belonged together and it never occurred to me that there could ever be a debate over which form of expression was more important.

These experiences were just a few that followed me throughout my life as an educator and scholar seeking to understand how the history of Black literate traditions evolved and where these traditions fit within a larger framework for research in language, literacy, and culture. In my quest to understand historical and contemporary perspectives of Black literate lives I begin with the concept of institution-building not only because this ideology was part of my foundation but because Independent Black Institutions embody the dynamic relationship Black people in many contexts have had with reading, writing, speaking, thinking, and action. Independent Black Institutions did not begin with the emergence of the Black Power and Black Arts Movements; institution-building for people of African descent in the context of the United States began during the enslavement of African people in the Americas. Wherever people could gather, they created their own institutions for teaching and learning. Later those who gathered would find refuge in churches, beauty parlors, private homes and most recently cafés/coffee houses, bookstores, and mixed-use performance spaces. At the core of all of these institutions was literacy. However, it is critical to note that the Black Arts Movement was decidedly committed to the building and maintenance of institutions.

Other scholars may choose to begin elsewhere and many have; for where does one begin to examine the literacy practices of Black people when recovery work reveals there is still more data to be mined? It is critical to state that Black lives, and therefore the literacy practices of Black people, are not monolithic. Where I choose to begin may not reflect the choices of others nor does my research undermine theirs. For example, educational researchers have rigorously examined critical aspects of Black literate lives such as the emergence of literary societies after slavery and during Reconstruction (McHenry, 2002; McHenry & Heath, 1994); the role of slave narratives and contemporary narratives and the philosophical underpinnings of African American education (Perry, 2003); the African Diaspora worldview of language and literacy (Smitherman, 1999); the evolution of African American Vernacular English or AAVE (Baugh, 1983, Rickford & Rickford, 2000, Ball, 1995; Ball & Lardner, 2005) as well as how AAVE can be used to help African American students use prior knowledge to develop literary reasoning skills (Lee, 1995, 2006, 2007). Additionally, contemporary perspectives have examined the influences of hip hop in African American literacy practices (Richardson, 2006; Alim and Baugh, 2006). Educational research, however, is limited in its treatment of Black writers, poets, and their institutions in school and in out-of-school contexts that specifically focused the self-determination and self-reliance of Black youth, their families, and teachers made critically important in the 1960s and 1970s. Institution-building that guided the Black Power and Black Arts Movements provide rich cultural maps for following the trajectory of literate practices among Blacks; such literate practices not only extended communal values established during the enslavement of Africans in the Americas but also forged new traditions of literacy activism and advocacy.

Here I take what may appear to be a departure from this narrative in order to contextualize the ideology of the Black Power and Black Arts Movements. Scholars and historians typically view the birth of the Black Power Movement in June 1966 during the James Meredith March or the "March Against Fear" (Joseph, 2006b; Collins & Crawford, 2006). As the first person to integrate the University of Mississippi, James Meredith bravely decided to walk through Mississippi in hopes "to embolden black Mississippians" who were consistently terrorized by whites who were resistant to integration (Collins & Crawford, 2006, p. 3). The tenor of the march changed when Meredith was shot by a white sniper and Civil Rights workers responded by converging on his home state in order to complete the journey on his behalf. A decidedly non-violent philosophy that guided the Student Nonviolent Coordinating Committee (SNCC) was replaced with Stokely Carmichael's—the chairman of SNCC—"defiant declaration" that became known to the world as "Black Power!" (Joseph, 2006b, p. xii).

Recent scholarship has introduced new perspectives on the Black Power and Black Arts Movements. In his study, *Waiting 'til the midnight hour: A narrative history of the Black Power Movement in America*, Joseph asserts: "Black Power, beginning with its revision of black identity, transformed America's racial, social, and political landscape. In a premulticultural age where race shaped hope, opportunity, and identity, Black Power provided new words, images, and politics" (p. xiv). The widely embraced Civil Rights Movement often casts a dark shadow over the Black Power Movement which has experienced a "character assassination," according to poet Amiri Baraka, from both Blacks and white critics for being divisive in nature. New studies demonstrate the overlap of these movements while also repositioning the contributions the Black Power and eventually Black Arts Movement made to the rising consciousness and education of Black people. However, even in these groundbreaking studies, the role of literacy is vital but, as presented, it is not central. Joseph casts the usual and not so usual suspects as "forerunners" in this often misunderstood struggle for Black dignity. In tracing Malcolm Little's journey from Omaha, Nebraska and Michigan to Malcolm X's ministry in Harlem mosques and on Harlem streets, Joseph's narrative implicitly demonstrates the movement's relationship with literacy. For example, one of Malcolm X's mentors, advisors, and supporters was Lewis Michaux who owned Michaux's National Memorial Bookstore in Harlem. Michaux's bookstore, also known as the "House of Common Sense" and the "Home of Proper Propaganda," doubled as a stage, podium, and pulpit for Malcolm X who used the sidewalk and space in front of the store to deliver sermons and speeches. Mr. Michaux himself was a member of Marcus Garvey's United Negro Improvement Association (UNIA) which is considered one of the first mass Black Nationalist movements. For a bookstore owner to be invested in the lives of people in his or her community speaks to the dialectical relationship between literacy and activism among Blacks in the context of the United States. In return, artists and political leaders understood the power and centrality of community institutions like bookstores in building relationships and establishing forums to exchange information.

Additional links between the Black Power Movement and the literate and literary practices of Black people were evident in arts and theatre. Joseph asserts that Lorraine Hansberry's play *A Raisin in the Sun*, which debuted on Broadway as Malcolm X was igniting the flames of Black self-determination uptown, "trumpeted the arrival of a cultural nationalism destined to be associated almost exclusively with Black Power militants" (Joseph, 2006b, p. 28). *A Raisin in the Sun*, a title that honored and signified Langston Hughes' poem "Harlem," told the story of a Black family from the South Side of Chicago and their struggles with racism and classism. Hansberry, according to Joseph, was a part of the Harlem Writers Guild along with other writers like John Oliver Killens; Harlem writers in the 1950s were courageously synthesizing their work with politics and setting the stage for artists of the Black Arts Movement. In the same way writers were moving into the fiery discourse on race, Black jazz musicians and actors were too. Jazz vocalist Abbey Lincoln and jazz drummer Max Roach transformed their New York penthouse into a literary salon for Harlem writers by hosting gatherings in their honor. Roach's album *We Insist! Max Roach's Freedom Now Suite* was not just a nod to the movement but part of his lifelong contributions to the struggle for social justice in America. "Freedom now" was also a phrase that was popular and seen in its Kiswahili translation, "Uhuru Sasa." Indeed, Max Roach and Abbey Lincoln performed at IBIs like the EAST in Brooklyn for free in order to raise money for their school also named Uhuru Sasa which I discuss further in Chapter 3. Actors Ossie Davis and his wife Ruby Dee were equally supportive of art embracing politics and were known supporters of Malcolm X's uncompromising demands for Black self-reliance. Artists, along with members of groups like Congress On Racial Equality (CORE) and SNCC, were entering the same domain:

> Inspired by the late Malcolm X's call for collective definition, self-determination, self-reliance, self-respect, and self-defense, these resolute activists began to call for racial solidarity and black pride, independent black leadership and freedom from white authority and, in some cases, armed defense and/or struggle under the rubric of "Black Power."
> (Collins & Crawford, 2006, p. 4)

When Malcolm X was assassinated on February 21, 1965 in Harlem's Audubon Ballroom, poet and playwright LeRoi Jones left his life in the East Village where he enjoyed acclaim for his writing, to move to Harlem. Jones' objective at that moment was to launch the Black Arts Repertory Theater and School (BARTS) which became a launch pad for many writers, poets, and artists. Jones, who I always thought was one of my distant relatives since his framed and matted photo hung on our wall among other family members, became known as the father of the Black Arts Movement. Jones' announcement of the creation of BARTS just one day after Malcolm X's assassination became a prophetic precursor to Black writers who catapulted themselves into the struggle for Black solidarity. Larry Neal, theorist and scholar who Jones referred to as the "spiritual leader" of the Black Arts Movement, considered this movement to be one of the branches of Black nationalism. In his essay simply entitled "The Black Arts Movement," Neal asserts:

> Black Art is the aesthetic and spiritual sister of the Black Power concept. As such, it envisions an art that speaks directly to the needs and aspirations of Black America . . . The Black Arts and Black Power concept both relate broadly to the Afro-American's desire for self determination and nationhood.
>
> (Neal, 1971, p. 272)

Neal went on to project that Black artists would begin "to define the world in their own terms." Art and artistry, however, would not be enough. To be sure, Neal argued that "Poetry is a concrete function, an action. No more abstractions" (p. 276). In his analysis of the "Black radical imagination," Kelley posits that poetry "is not what we simply recognize as the formal 'poem,' but a revolt: a scream in the night, an emancipation of language and old ways of thinking" (2002, p. 9). Poets and writers like LeRoi Jones, Sonia Sanchez, Don L. Lee, Nikki Giovanni, Kalamu ya Salaam became educators and many opened their own schools to give shape to their vision of the future.

Mapping the Continuum

Chapter 1 is at once ambitious but not exhaustive. In this chapter I review recovery work on African American literacy practices as well as historiographies of education and self-reliance among Black readers, writers, and speakers beginning with the enslavement of Africans in the Americas. In this first chapter I move towards a theory of African American literacy practices that not only focuses on reading, writing, and speaking but also how literacy leads to activism and how activism then re-informs literacy to form a dialectical relationship.

In order to demonstrate the ways in which Black readers, writers, and speakers build institutions that move beyond speaking words to active engagement, I turn to the life of Gwendolyn Brooks in Chapter 2. I examine Brooks's evolution from "Negro poet" to "Black poet" to demonstrate the links between literacy and activism. While there are numerous Black poets and writers who are activists, I chose Brooks because of her dramatic shift in thinking about her work in relationship to her people. Brooks is very strategic about announcing her shift from being solely a writer who crafts words to being a writer who crafts Black lives. Brooks's career as a poet is undeniably one of the most impressive as evidenced by her countless awards and honors. However, little attention has been paid to the impact that Brooks's strategic and purposeful shift in her poet identity had on her own writing and her work with emerging Black writers. I argue that Brooks's post-1967 discourse and new identity were manifested in her "pedagogy of possibility" in which she used her writing and life experiences to incite and challenge a new generation of writers and teachers.

Brooks's decision to publish her writing with Black presses in spite of the fact that she would not make as much money and quite possibly have some of her works not be as accessible signaled the strategic and purposeful movement towards Independent Black Institutions (IBIs). IBIs were not, of course, limited to publishing houses. They also influenced the dissemination of information and education. In Chapter 3, I continue to examine the role of literacy activism and advocacy within the context of institution-building. More specifically I focus on *Black News* newspaper that came out of the EAST organization in Brooklyn, New York City. *Black News* was founded in 1969 in response to the Ocean Hill-Brownville struggle for community control of public schools. This chapter examines how institution-building in the late 1960s and 1970s sought to address the "miseducation" of Black youth in public schools and re-educate their families, and teachers. Ultimately, Chapter 3 demonstrates how *Black News* redefined literacy to include issues in education and politics as well as music, art, and promote overall well-being.

IBIs that have inspired poets and writers like Brooks and the creation of newspapers such as *Black News* have also inspired twenty-first-century Black institutions primarily committed to the circulation and preservation of written and spoken words. I have referred to these contemporary institutions as Participatory Literacy Communities (PLCs). PLCs such as

Black-owned and operated bookstores and spoken word poetry events operate with the same values of self-reliance found in traditional IBIs while cultivating new and experienced readers, writers, speakers, and lovers of the word. In Chapter 4, I revisit my study of two Black-owned and operated bookstore events and two spoken word poetry "open mic" events in Northern California.

PLCs are not limited to out-of-school sites. In Chapter 5, I demonstrate how IBIs have come full circle by examining the work of a poet/teacher, Mama C, literacy activism, and her community of student poets and writers in an urban public high school in Brooklyn, New York. I also demonstrate how the symbol of fire seen throughout Black literary traditions and struggles lives on through the work of Mama C and her students. Using strategies that helped her develop a literate identity in the 1960s and 1970s, Mama C introduced poetry and history to students in the hope of cultivating the next generation of poet-writer-activists.

This book reinterprets historiographies of Black self-determination and self-reliance by focusing on the role of literacy. Ultimately I hope to make visible the layers of the written and spoken word and their relationship to self-determination and empowerment. In their shift from readers, writers, and speakers to "doers," literacy activists and advocates build a bridge between these histories and contemporary portrayals.

CHAPTER 1

Toward a Theory of Black Literate Lives

In order to contribute to a theoretical framework for understanding the literate practices of African people in the context of the United States, I draw from scholarship examining Black readers, writers, speakers, and activists of the early 1800s. Any viable framework must be viewed tentatively because new discoveries are still being made. Therefore, scholars interested in such work cannot "theorize in a totalizing fashion" (Peterson, 1995, p. 4). Enslaved and freed Blacks participated in the teaching and learning of literacy unbeknownst to slave owners who opposed education for Blacks in general. Literacy efforts included secret schools, and literary societies that emerged during Reconstruction as well as speakers and writers who used oral and written texts to confront racial oppression. Recovery work has demonstrated how these institutions created literate traditions "to supplement and sustain their literary education" (McHenry, 2002, p. 10). Additionally, research examining lives of Blacks in the early nineteenth and twentieth centuries reveals the intersection between reading, writing, speaking, and action. To be sure, in a study of "'Doers" of the word, Peterson (1995) posits that for African American women speakers and writers "speaking and writing constituted a form of doing, of social action, continuous with their social, political, and cultural work" (p. 3). Peterson's analysis of women speakers and writers could also be used while examining male writers, and speakers such as Frederick Douglass and David Walker. In sum, early literacy practices were not solely carried out for the purpose of leisure and enjoyment but they were political acts that could be considered early forms of institution-building. Literacy always served a greater purpose and it was that purpose that drove the craftsmanship of language and activism.

Arguing that institutions "are frequently viewed as cumbersome bureaucracies," Peterson contextualizes the need for Blacks as well as other subaltern groups to build their own institutions in order to resist unjust practices (p. 11). In an examination of Independent Black Institutions (IBIs), and African-centered schools in particular, Lee (1992) asserts "institutions validate knowledge, help to shape visions, inculcate values, and provide the foundation for community stability" (p. 161). Lee argued that the establishment of Black educational institutions was critical because of the "dismal failure" of the education of African American children in American public schools. Indeed, the word "institution" can conjure images of something detached and impersonal such as non-descript buildings that house perfunctory transactions. However, "institutions" in the context of Black literate lives are not merely stages to play out predictable roles or actions—rather they constitute a collective consciousness of values and ideologies sometimes carried in the minds and hearts of its participants in the absence of formal buildings or recognition from the dominant culture of power. Scholarship focusing on the literate practices of Black people pre-supposes the inextricable link between institution-building and power:

> [Institutions] have often provided subordinate groups with a means to power: they create organized consent among their members by means of specific cultural, social, and intellectual activities; they work to promote the welfare of the population as a whole over that of specific individuals or groups; they encourage the powerful planning of resistance strategies; they make public and thus more effective hitherto privately held sentiments.
>
> (Peterson, 1995, p. 11)

Peterson and Lee's scholarship redirects the notion of institutions solely as bureaucratic and repositions them as a catalyst for subaltern groups to establish far-reaching forums for organizing around specific purposes and goals. According to Lee, the purpose of IBIs that focused on teaching and learning was "to educate and socialize African American children to assume their future roles as political, intellectual, spiritual and economic leaders in their community" (1992, p. 161). In sum, churches, schools, newspapers, bookstores are institutions that have afforded Black people opportunities to preserve literate traditions while cultivating future leaders. This is one of the foremost purposes of IBIs and for good reason. In an analysis on how curriculum is influenced by ideology, Apple (2004) asserts the "ahistorical nature of education" in the context of United States makes it far too easy to forget how schools sought to assimilate Black and Latino youth, thus marginalizing if not outright devaluing these students' familial and community contributions (p. 63). Family and community contributions of Black people honored the word in all its forms. IBIs honored the histories of Black children while unapologetically encouraging cultural pride. The aim of this chapter is to provide a framework for examining the literate practices of people of African Americans in the early forms of institution-building. By surveying the history of self-determination in the quest for education and thus literacy and by revisiting the orality and literacy debates in educational research, this chapter will demonstrate how written text has served as a "call" in the lives and culture of Black people.

"Stealin' and Meetin'": A Self-determined Education

Literacy is and will continue to be at the core of understanding the lives of Black people in the United Sates. The outlawing of literacy for enslaved Africans established the relationships between literacy, power, and humanity or as Ladson-Billings (2005) argues "literacy is deeply embedded in our conceptions of humanity early on in the construction of the United States and citizenship; that is, one must be human to be literate and one must be literate to be a citizen" (p. 135). Therefore slave holders had to keep literacy beyond the reach of those whom they enslaved; to do otherwise would be acknowledging the men and women who were being used as chattel were indeed human. Scholars have used the tenuous relationship between literacy and humanity during the enslavement of Africans as a precursor to understanding an African American philosophy of learning (Perry, 2003). In a close reading of slave narratives and twentieth-century autobiographies and memoirs, Perry showed how themes of literacy and liberation were consistent across texts and revealed that teaching and learning literacy were often depicted as a "communal act" that valued reciprocity among the stories of Black people:

> While learning to read was an individual achievement, it was fundamentally a communal act. For the slaves, literacy affirmed not only their individual freedom but also the freedom of their people. Becoming literate obliged one to teach others. Learning and teaching were two sides of the same coin, part of the same moment. Literacy was not something you kept for yourself; it was to be passed on to others, to the community. Literacy was something to share.
>
> (p. 14)

Perry explicated the narratives of Frederick Douglass, Harriet Jacobs, Malcolm X, Jocelyn Elders, Don L. Lee (Haki Madhubuti), and others. Douglass's 1845 autobiography is one of the best-known accounts of Black people's struggle for literacy under the watchful gaze of the peculiar institution. Douglass learned how powerful literacy was after witnessing the fury of his slave master when Mr. Auld discovered his wife was teaching a young Douglass to read. Douglass recounted that "from that moment, I understood the pathway from slavery to freedom" (Douglass, 1968, p. 47). According to Douglass, the reaction of Mr. Auld drove him to learn to read and write by any means necessary. While the value of slave narratives should never be underestimated, scholars like Peterson and McHenry have asserted that slave narratives do not provide a complete picture. Peterson (1995) further argues that holding these narratives up as models has profound consequences:

> As a result, literary criticism of the late twentieth century has come dangerously close to replicating the historical situation of the early nineteenth century in its valorization of those African American texts produced under the direction of white sponsors for the consumption of a white readership, while marginalizing and even occluding those other forms of narrative writing produced for the black community.
>
> (p. 5)

Peterson's critique of the historical portrayals of literacy in the lives of Black people closes in on one of the prevailing debates in educational research and literacy research in particular: What is literacy? Who gets counted among the literate and what literate practices and institutions are valued? Most importantly, which stories get told and who are the key players in the construction of Black literacy? This is particularly important in the field of education where "struggles over the curriculum—over whose experience would be represented as valid or whose language or history would be taught—are unquestionably long-standing" (Buras and Apple, 2006, p. 24). Communities associated with orality are far too often regarded with less respect than communities that privilege the written word. Peterson also cautions against the omission of spoken and written texts specifically for Black people with the intention to build institutions that define values and promote self-reliance. Using the writings of N.F. Mossell, Peterson contends that scholars must consider a wide range of "texts" (including poetry, journalisms, fiction, and history) as well as look outside of "texts as pure objects" and consider the sociopolitical contexts in which texts, both oral and written, have been produced. I will address this crucial point later in this chapter (Peterson, 1995, p. 5).

In addition to including a wide range of texts in the definition of literacy, the theme of community and self-determination is consistent across scholarship and recovery work on Black readers, writers, and speakers. Tracing the "Black struggle for literacy" during the nineteenth century, Holt (1990) argues that the goal of education for Black Americans was "social as well as personal improvement to uplift the people, to make conditions better" (p. 93). Referencing accounts of enslaved Africans, Holt explains that the irony of beatings administered by slave masters to their slaves who dared to become literate reinforced the importance of education like the aforementioned narrative of Frederick Douglass. Although there are accounts of slave owners who taught their slaves some reading, writing, and math skills, Holt highlights the contributions of Black men and women who held "secret schools" in which they passed on whatever reading and writing skills they had to others. Oftentimes, these schools were without walls and assembled wherever you had an able teacher and willing student. Holt noted that white northern missionaries are often documented as the major contributors to African American education. While acknowledging these "heroic" efforts, Holt maintains that there is a lack of scholarship that shows the determination of African Americans to educate themselves. Holt referred to the educational system established by Blacks after slavery as a "chain letter of instruction" (p. 94); men, women, and children shared the little information they had with each other and continued to pass it on. During the Civil War and particularly the period of Reconstruction, Black teachers often conducted their own classes in "self-help schools" with whatever material and space they had. According to Gutman (1987), sometimes a "cellar" or an abandoned "old school-house" was used as a classroom. Even if the teacher was "an old negro in spectacles" or "a colored woman, who as a family servant had some privileges" (p. 270), he or she shared whatever literacy skills they had with other black people. Former slaves actively sought educational opportunities for their children (Morris, 1981).[1] From these accounts, we can trace how a tradition of reading, writing, and speaking became a part of "doing" as well. In other words, part of becoming "literate" was to assume the responsibility to contribute to one's immediate and at-large community.

In his seminal study on the Black struggle for education in the South, 1865–1930, Anderson (1988) traces the self-determination of Blacks, both enslaved and free, to ensure a universal education. Much like Peterson's concern that late twentieth-century literary criticism omitted the work of Blacks done for Blacks, Anderson notes that Black "self-determination" for education is often absent from scholarly work. In Anderson's findings, literacy is not only synonymous with education but it is often considered the gateway to freedom and the foundation of institutions for the next generations. Anderson's research emphasized the role of literacy in the pursuit of universal education by noting, "Blacks emerged from slavery with a strong belief in the desirability of learning to read and write." The determined efforts of Black people in this movement illustrated their "belief in the value of literate culture" (p. 5). Anderson demonstrated that Black people in the South were engaged in "self-teaching" prior to Abraham Lincoln's Emancipation Proclamation in 1863 or the estab-lishment of the Freedman's Bureau of 1865. In sum, "slaves and free persons of color had already begun to make plans for the systematic instruction of their illiterates" (p. 7).

Consistent with Perry's examination of a philosophy of education for Blacks, Anderson showed that literacy was central to the movement for universal education and the catalyst for maintaining "communal values" (p. 9). For example, Sabbath Schools, or largely church-sponsored schools that held classes on weekends and evenings, were committed to educating countless numbers of Blacks. However, prior to Sabbath

Schools and other self-help schools, informal networks demonstrated early promises of institution-building among Blacks. "Stealin' and Meetin'" were collectives of free Blacks returning to teach enslaved Blacks to read. There were also Blacks who refused to be uneducated and illiterate; "rebel literates," according to Anderson, "viewed literacy and formal education as a means to liberation and freedom" (p. 17). Education wasn't a means to an end; it was the planting of a seed that would eventually blossom into a mass movement toward independence for Blacks. Black educators, according to Anderson, "insisted that ex-slaves must educate themselves" in order to "acquire a responsible awareness of duties as citizens . . . education could help raise a freed people to an appreciation of their historic responsibility to develop a better society" (p. 28).

The "ethos of education and literacy" (Franklin, 1994) continued to be at the heart of institution-building for people of African descent. Reading, writing, and speaking had to have a purpose which is why they often encircled each other. There was no time for a hierarchy for a people on a mission to educate youth and reeducate elders. The next section seeks to frame the implications for these historiographies of education and literacy and what they tell about the role of words both spoken and written, in the building of independent black institutions.

"I Can Read De People": Orality and Literacy

Literacy research has engaged the orality/literacy debate, or what has been referred to as the "great divide," for decades. Early scholarship explored the technology of writing and its contributions to language and cognition (Scribner and Cole, 1981; Ong, 2001; Olson, 2001) as well as the relationship between literacy and education or schooling (Graff, 2001; Cook-Gumperz, 2006). For example, Ong's study of writing as a technology argues that the term "illiterate" is problematic in that it "suggests that persons belonging to the class it designates are deviants, defined by something they lack, namely literacy" (p. 19). Ong further asserts that "literates" are often distressed by orality because of their desire to "pin down" events whereas the orally trained mind "can operate with exquisite skill in the world of sounds, events, evanescences" (p. 20). Other scholars have argued that the tool of writing has significantly contributed to cognition and learning. In "Writing and the mind," Olson (1995/2001) argues that humans in many ways owe their "intellectual debt" to the written word or "scripts." While these studies offer important perspectives in the history of writing and reading, they also reify a dichotomous relationship between orality and literacy. Perhaps one of the most valuable contributions to these debates that pushed scholarship to consider multiple ways of being literate is Scribner and Cole's study of the Vai people in Liberia (2001). To be sure, Scribner and Cole reported that the Vai people had three "scripts" that contributed to how literacy was defined in the context of their communities. The Vai had their own script which was largely used for personal communication, Arabic script for religious purposes, and English script which was considered "official" for both politics and economics (p. 129). Scribner and Cole used their findings to refute the notion of a monolithic view of writing and the outcomes of writing. In the history of American education those who stood on the wrong side of the "great divide" were disadvantaged once literacy became central to schooling (Graff, 1987/2001). In a study of the nineteenth-century origins of literacy, Graff argues that in the context of the United States, "education was associated with respectability and advancement." Graff further asserts, "social and cultural needs for literacy, however, while growing in number and import, continued to compete with the needs of daily life, survival, and popular recreations— for these literacy was not often central" (p. 215). This divide has continued to draw lines between who is counted as respectable as well as who was considered undeserving in American public schools. McHenry and Heath assert that the creation of "cultural logos" to define various ethnic groups in the context of the United States has "served academic culture by allowing the distancing and objectifying of African Americans while reserving designations such as 'literate' for the 'dominant' culture" (McHenry and Heath, 1994, p. 263). In order to complicate these designations, McHenry and Heath examine the literate practices of people of African descent in which "speaking encircled reading, and how reading—especially of literature—surrounded writing" (p. 265). McHenry and Heath as well as a more comprehensive study conducted by McHenry (2002) show how the literate practices of people of African descent blur boundaries between oral and literate designations.

One of the most unfortunate omissions from this historical debate in educational research is an analysis of the oral and literate practices of people of African descent. Orality and literacy work together in Black literary productions—an idea that I return to before the end of this chapter. In a study on African American vernacular poetry, Brown addresses the orality/literacy debate: "The African American writer centers a speaking voice in a written text very often through the presentation of a dramatic scenario. Similarly, African American vernacular culture manifests itself in the realms of orality and literacy" (Brown, 1999, p. 28).

Isabella Bomfree, better known as Sojourner Truth, personifies the problem in dichotomizing oral and literate practices. Born in 1797 to parents who were enslaved, Bomfree would not experience freedom until she "took" it approximately one year before emancipation. In the mid-nineteenth century, Truth traveled throughout the United States to speak against the institution of slavery. According to historians, Truth was by all accounts "illiterate"—that is, she was unable to read and write. In fact, some of what is known about Truth's life comes from the "ethno-biography" tradition which is an autobiography for people who are unable to "write." Peterson posits that the tradition of the ethno-biography "forces us to come to terms with the difficulty of recognizing and naming that which lies on the other side of writing" (Peterson, 1995, p. 45). Truth's use of speech to organize others challenges traditional notions of what it means to be a writer. Peterson asserts that Truth understood "both the power of written language to authorize and interpret experiences and her exclusion from this arena of power" (1995, p. 39). To be sure, Truth questioned the authority of the written word noting, "I can't read a book, but I can read de people" (Gilbert and Titus, p. 216, in Peterson, p. 39). In sum, Peterson argues that Truth was still able to make use of the technologies of writing even though she was not able to participate in the practice of writing in the traditional sense: "It was [Truth's] very lack of literacy that made possible her appropriation of different modes of 'writing' and enabled her to enter 'modernity'; no longer 'primitive,' she must be marked as 'modern'" (p. 39).

Sojourner Truth forces scholars and literacy theorists to reconsider the contributions that people of African descent have made to literacy as well as what counts for literacy. Reading the people, a skill Truth was proud to possess, has been one of the most important functions of literacy for Black people in the context of the United States and was in alignment with the communal value of literacy teaching and learning. Truth embodied the spirit of self-determination that guided enslaved Africans in their quest for education and literacy.

Navigating the Word, the Text and the "Call"

> Men of colour, who are also of sense, for you particularly is my APPEAL designed. Our more ignorant brethren are not able to penetrate its value. I call upon you therefore to cast your eyes upon the wretchedness of your brethren, and to do your utmost to enlighten them—go to work and enlighten your brethren!
>
> (From David Walker's *Appeal*, [1830] 1993)

Perhaps one of the most powerful illustrations of words inciting action in the nineteenth century is David Walker's *Appeal*. Walker's pamphlet published in 1830 was not only a "petition against slavery" but also a text with "factual density and richly constructed arguments for freedom" (Turner, 1993, p. 10). Walker's *Appeal*, which carried the subtitle "To the Coloured Citizens of the World, but in particular, and very expressly, to those of the United States of America," had such power among enslaved and free Blacks that slavery apologists frequently used adjectives like "incendiary" and "subversive" to describe it. Walker himself was born "free" on September 28, 1785, in Wilmington, North Carolina. According to scholar James Turner the status of children born to slaves was determined by the mother's status in the state of North Carolina. Walker's mother was "free"—an unusual scenario to say the least—while his father remained enslaved.

Walker's "free" status afforded him opportunities to travel throughout the United States where he inevitably witnessed the violence and oppression of slavery. Eventually Walker settled in Boston in 1826 where he established a clothing business. It was during this period that Walker ardently studied which became the foundation for the *Appeal*. The publication, which Turner contends was a synthesis of presentations, speeches, and written text, was funded by Walker's business. Walker's experience as a Boston agent for the abolitionist journal *Freedom's Journal* was possibly useful in conceptualizing how the *Appeal* would be disseminated. In the "Preamble" to the *Appeal*, Walker addresses those who can read as well as those who cannot;

> It is expected that all coloured men, women and children, of every nation, language, tongue under heaven, will try to procure a copy of this *Appeal* and read it, or get someone to read it to them, for it is designed more particularly for them.
>
> (Walker, [1830] 1993, p. 20)

By acknowledging readers as well as non-readers Walker implicitly uses his appeal to reinforce the value of reciprocity among Blacks in the teaching and learning of literacy. Walker's *Appeal*, organized in four articles along with the Preamble, urged Blacks to work in solidarity to eradicate slavery even if it meant bearing arms. Walker also argued for the need for more education, noting "the major part of white Americans, have, ever since we have been among them, tried to keep us ignorant" (p. 54). Walker was so insistent and passionate in his language that his pamphlet was feared among slaveholders. McHenry (2002) asserted that once the *Appeal* reached Savannah, Georgia, legislators representing Georgia and Louisiana not only ceased distribution of this charge for Blacks to take their freedom but they also "enacted laws to control and prevent Black literacy" (p. 31). Most central to the purpose of this book is the fact that Walker's written text was created—to borrow McHenry's terms—to embolden and empower all Black people regardless of literate or illiterate status:

> It is important to note that for Walker the imperative that the literate read the *Appeal* to the illiterate was not a straightforward endorsement of the already-scripted Western idea that those without literacy skills were also without logic . . . Rather than viewing literacy exclusively as a sign of an elevated state of reason, Walker recognized it as a powerful apparatus that might be deployed in various ways by black Americans to further their pursuit of civil rights.
>
> (p. 36)

McHenry's observations support the aforementioned discussion of self-determination and the self-reliance among Blacks in their pursuit of education and literacy. The investment in literacy as a "communal value" refutes an oral/written dichotomy; there was not time for sorting people based on ability when revolutionary action was needed to ensure freedom and civil rights. Walker's *Appeal* is not only said to be a precursor to slave revolts that followed its publication and distribution but also to Black Nationalist movements such as Marcus Garvey and the Black Power and Black Arts Movements. Walker has also been historicized as a "philosophical and spiritual father" of activists such as Garvey, Malcolm X, Ella Baker, Assata Shakur, and many others (Turner, 1993, p. 18).

Marcus Garvey built the first Pan African Nationalist movement through his Universal Negro Improvement Association (UNIA). While Garvey's accomplishments through UNIA are vast, here I focus specifically on his newspaper *The Negro World*, which sought to bring together thoughts and ideas in poetry and prose from people of African descent who were committed to racial uplift—that is, Black people building and sustaining institutions for economic development and education. If Walker served as a foundation to Garvey's movement, Garvey was a "fitting precursor" to the Black Power and Black Arts Movements in that he "preached race pride, community control, self-reliance and, in a word, Black nationalism" (Martin, 1983, p. 2). In his seminal study *Literary Garveyism: Garvey, Black Arts, and the Harlem Renaissance*, Martin argues that Garvey's contributions to the literary scene are often undermined if not entirely omitted. Martin carefully traces Garvey's passion for poetry, literature, music, and elocution. Garvey's *Negro World* served as an institution for philosophical debates as well as a forum to get poetry back to the people. Arguing that most Garveyites were poets, including Garvey himself, Martin asserts, "Theirs for the most part was a fighting poetry, the poetry of an oppressed people who would be free" (pp. 44–45). Poetry was a part of *Negro World* from its first printing in 1918 and was central to the newspaper throughout its existence. One section in particular, "Poetry for the People"—a name that would live on through the life and work of poet and activist June Jordan—celebrated the poetic efforts of the *Negro World* readership.[2]

On the pages of *Negro World*, poetry was not written merely to entertain and Garvey in particular "used his poetry to expound his political ideas, to document his struggles, to express his private emotions" (p. 139). Walker and Garvey's contributions to Black self-reliance not only employed oral and literate strategies but also depended on their fusion. Members of Garvey's UNIA were expected to participate in public debates, encouraged to take elocution classes and attend lectures at the 135th Street Harlem branch of the New York City Public Library (now the Schomburg). UNIA frequently hosted music concerts and had their own choir, band, and orchestra. The *Negro World* then was a forum where UNIA members and readers were "able to supplement its interest in writing with access to some of the best spoken word" (p. 120).

Arguing that writing extends from aspects of orality such as speaking and singing, Brown (1999) asserts that African American poetry and writing were typically composed for the purposes of sharing aloud. According to Brown, the written is dependent on the spoken:

> The African American poet uses scriptings as a way to communicate voicings. Writing is an extension of speaking or singing. African world cultures value word skills, poetry making, storytelling, and the literary extensions of these more public activities; they rely on an audience that is hearing as well as reading.
>
> (p. 29)

If we considered Brown's analysis of how African American poets and writers work, there would be important educational implications for the teaching of literacy. At the very least we would find it useless to continuously dichotomize "oral" and "literate" practices. On a practical level, we would extend opportunities for students to utilize multiple forms of expression if they were helpful to their composition process. Furthermore, Brown's analyses shifts the focus to the importance of *purpose* in such writing; the emphasis of the audience possessing a key role in the production and performance of African American poetry presupposes that the composer/performer has to have something he or she believes is important enough to be shared aloud. Brown describes African American orature as having a "double consciousness" to signify the work of W.E.B. Dubois. According to Brown's theory, it would seem that people of African descent do not merely straddle "orality" and "literacy," but that orality is a major force for literacy; it is the spoken word that gets heard by the community. Brown's argument is evidenced in the cases of David Walker, Marcus Garvey, and Sojourner Truth.

In this chapter I traced the unfolding of IBIs beginning with the efforts of enslaved Africans to recreate the three Rs to include reading, writing, and reciprocity. I argue that literacy, that is reading, writing, and speaking, were not a means to an ends but driven by purpose and propelled by a desire for a people to become independent and self-sufficient. Former slaves became teachers in out-of-school contexts due to the urgency of creating networks for disseminating information. Because of the varying skills among Black men and women, the readers were responsible for the non-readers as David Walker's *Appeal* demonstrates. Words were for mobilizing and organizing or as Truth underscored, it was "reading the people" that counted the most. In sum, Black literate practices demonstrate a dialectic relationship between the word—both spoken and written—with forms of social protest and literacy activism. In the next chapter, I focus on the life and work of Gwendolyn Brooks. Brooks, a poet and later an activist, used her writing to create a pedagogy of possibility for emerging readers and writers. Brooks's life best illustrates how poets and writers during the 1960s and 1970s embraced the literacy activism of their enslaved forefathers and foremothers.

CHAPTER 2

"I Don't Want Us to Forget the Fire"

The Literacy Activism of Gwendolyn Brooks

In an analysis of the poetry and music of the "the movement," Harding (1990) argues that Black poets in the late 1960s were at the forefront of the struggle for democracy throughout the United States:

> Poets became community leaders, organizers, publishers, mobilizers, political forces, as well as healers. Almost all became leaders of writing workshops, extending the skills and gifts of their craft to others who were willing to receive, announcing thereby the fundamentally democratic nature of their art.
>
> (p. 134)

Harding's portrayal of these "poets, musicians, and magicians" who embraced opportunities to nurture new writers and potential leaders is evidenced in the literacy activism of Gwendolyn Brooks. Referred to as a "sorceress of sounds" (Madhubuti, 1974) and a "consummate portraitist" (Alexander, 2005), Brooks purposefully used her poet identity and writing to cultivate emerging Black writers. With arms outstretched, Gwendolyn Brooks's life and works not only embraced the Harlem Renaissance (Brooks met Langston Hughes as a teenager in Chicago and corresponded with James Weldon Johnson), as well as the era of protest literature, but also enfolded the work of younger poets in the Black Arts

Movement in the 1960s and beyond. Brooks championed a renaissance of her own by reappraising her own purpose for writing. This chapter seeks to examine how Brooks's literacy activism illustrates the blended traditions of reading, writing, orality, and social protest that were not only reflective of the Black Arts Movement but became a vital part of the struggle for Black self-reliance and self-determination. These connections were discussed in the previous chapter. Here, I will examine Brooks's discourse of reciprocity that she began to articulate as she experienced a tectonic shift from "Negro" poet to "Black" poet after attending the Second Annual Black Writers Conference in 1967 at Fisk University. By embracing the ideology of the Black Arts Movement which was fueled by the Black Power Movement, Brooks developed a "newish-Gwendolynian" voice in her poetry and herself. Brooks committed herself to the doctrine that Black poets and writers ought to write for and about Black people everywhere. Brooks has consistently identified the year 1967 as a turning point in her career. An examination of Gwendolyn Brooks's early life and her first experiences with writing and literature demonstrates how Brooks's strategic shift from "Negro" poet, to "Black" poet as evidenced in her post-1967 discourse helped shape her pedagogy of possibility which I discuss later in this chapter. Brooks's literacy activism was not only found in her post-1967 writings but also in the workshops she organized for emerging writers and her deliberate commentary about the role and responsibilities of Black poets. Additionally, Brooks developed a methodology and framework for extending her poetry and other literate practices to all Black people. Such activities should be considered an early blueprint for what Irvine (2002) and Ladson-Billings (1997, 2001) have referred to as "culturally relevant pedagogy." Brooks noted:

> My aim, in my next future, is to write poems that will somehow successfully "call" [see Imamu Baraka's "SOS"] all black people: black people in taverns, black people in alleys, black people in gutters, schools, offices, factories, prisons, the consulate; I wish to reach black people in pulpits, black people in mines, on farms, on thrones.
>
> (1972, p. 183)

Brooks's goal was to take poetry back to the people much like Garvey and his followers and meet them wherever they were. Brooks also embraced the necessity of orality and the power of "reading the people" like Sojourner Truth as she strove to write poems that could inspire Black people in a range of public spaces as opposed to traditional literary settings. This kind of literacy activism required writing relevant poetry that could be accessible to all. Brooks enjoyed a successful and consistent publishing career with Harper and Row (Harper and Brothers at that time) before she decided to move her work to Black publishing companies such as Broadside Press in Detroit, Michigan, and eventually Third World Press in Chicago, Illinois:

> [Brooks] leaves the community of "established" writers and readers and takes her art to the people in Bronzevilles[1] all across the nation. She conducts poetry workshops, gives public readings, establishes literary awards, and works in myriad ways to help bring into existence a second generation of black poets and to strengthen Black publishers.
>
> (Gayles, 2003, p. xv)

Brooks's life and body of work represent an awakening in Black poets and writers' awareness in the 1960s. Black writers and artists were moving away from their creations being viewed as mere art for art's sake and toward politicizing their work. Associating art with liberation and upliftment, the words of Black poets and writers served as an "SOS," to borrow from poet, playwright, activist and co-father of the Black Arts Movement. It was Amiri Baraka who sounded the call, "Calling all black people . . . Wherever you are, calling you, urgent, come in . . ." It was a call for Black people to organize against injustice in all forms and create Independent Black Institutions to educate Black youth, families, and inculcate the values of self-reliance (Baraka, 1995/1991, p. 218). This development was remarkable when one considers that Brooks was born in an era when Black writers "were still confronted with the pressure . . . to effectively 'prove' their literacy—and, thus, their humanity through mastery of European forms" (Alexander, 2005, p. xvii). During Reconstruction, efforts to build IBIs and establish literate identities began to focus on literacy to prove one's value to society. The focus on literacy as a tool of empowerment and independence highlighted in the work of David Walker, Sojourner Truth and Marcus Garvey dimmed in the growing pressure to assimilate. Brooks, who was born in the early 1900s and part of the Great Migration to northern cities from the south, was not introduced to the discourse of Black pride until it caught her by surprise much later in her life.

The Next Paul Laurence Dunbar

In many ways there were aspects of Gwendolyn Brooks's early life that embodied the spirit of the Black Arts Movement; education and learning for Brooks never solely took place in schools and classrooms. Brooks's parents exposed her to literature at an early age and projected her future by crowning her the next Paul Laurence Dunbar. In the first installment of her autobiography, *Report from Part One*, Brooks recollects sitting at a desk her father was able to get from his job and being surrounded with her "Emily Books" and Paul Laurence Dunbar. "Emily" was a young Canadian girl whose adventures were chronicled in a series of stories. Dunbar, as a poet, was both admired and admonished by Blacks for his commitment to preserve Black speech patterns in his poetry. Brooks notes:

> Certainly up there, holding special delights for a writing girl, were the Emily books . . . Certainly also, to look down at me whenever I sat at the desk was Paul Laurence Dunbar. "*You*," my mother had announced, "are going to be the *lady* Paul Laurence Dunbar." I still own the Emily books and the "Complete Paul Laurence Dunbar."
>
> (Brooks, 1972, p. 56)

Though born in Topeka, Kansas, in 1917, Brooks emphasized she was a "Chicagoan" because she was raised in Chicago and attended Chicago Public Schools. Brooks's parents moved to Chicago from Topeka before Brooks was born and returned to Topeka for Brooks's mother to give birth before returning to Chicago with a three-week-old Gwendolyn. Brooks's father, David Anderson Brooks, was a man who literally went out of his way to complete high school. The son of a runaway slave, David Anderson Brooks studied at Fisk University for one year aspiring to be a doctor. Once in Chicago, Brooks's father worked various jobs including a position as a janitor at McKinley's music publishing company. Here, David Anderson Brooks was given music, old books, and various odds and ends discarded by the office. These discarded items were gems to the young poet's family including the aforementioned desk that belonged to a young Gwendolyn. Brooks's mother, Kezia Corine Wims, was a school teacher prior to moving to Chicago. Her parents were advocates of literacy and Brooks has recounted fond memories of spending time reading *Writer's Digest* and the *Harvard Classics* at home. At 13, Brooks became enthralled with the fact that she could access writers from near and far on the pages of *Writer's Digest* who, like her, "ached for the want of the right word" in their writing (p. 56). Brooks did not believe she was a very good writer as a child; however, her mother continued to encourage her: "She was positive that my future depended only upon time; time would take care of everything, and I would be published. She had more faith in me than I did" (Gayles, 2003, pp. 27–28). For example, when Brooks's mother learned that her daughter had writing potential, she decided that Brooks should not spend too much time with housework. Instead, her mother would enlist Brooks's father and brother to help her so that Brooks could focus on reading and writing. Brooks further noted that her mother "always admired people who read with expression" and encouraged Brooks to do recitations as part of the programming at Carter Temple Church (Brooks, 1972, p. 49) which is yet another positive valuation of the oral or shared word.[2] At 13 years old, Brooks had taken an interest in the activities in her neighborhood and decided to start her own newspaper using the neighborhood gossip:

> I did show a little enterprise. When I was thirteen I founded a newspaper titled *The Champlain Weekly News.* My mother helped me make copies of the paper, and I sold it to neighbors for a nickel apiece. It got so that the neighbors were very eager for the weekly news to arrive. Some people rather took to me because I would listen very eagerly to the neighborhood gossip . . . We rented out an apartment upstairs, and I would stand in the vestibule listening to all the life that went on up there. I think everyone was greatly relieved when I gave up my career as a newspaperwoman.
>
> (Gayles, 2003, p. 28)

Brooks's neighbors were relieved not because they did not support her aspirations to become a writer, but more so because they no longer had to worry about becoming the subject of one of her news stories. The tradition of serving as a reporter to her community seemed to guide the trajectory of Brooks's future work. Brooks's mother insisted that she carry some of her poems to give to Langston Hughes after attending a reading he gave at Metropolitan Community Church in Chicago in 1933:

> I met Langston Hughes when I was sixteen. When I went to Metropolitan Community Church to show him some of my poems at the behest of my mother who accompanied me and saw to it that I did this. He was most kind and read the poems right there after his reading and told me that I had talent and that I should keep writing.
>
> (*Black Books Bulletin,* 1974, p. 34)

Hughes, known for his profound love for Black people and youth in particular, was a model for Brooks in later years. The source of her admiration was Hughes's desire and willingness to mentor and advise young writers. Brooks also approached James Weldon Johnson during one of his readings in Chicago. Although Johnson was not as responsive as Hughes during their first face-to-face meeting, he had taken time to return Brooks's letters, praise her writing, and encourage her to seek out the work of modern poets. The feedback that Brooks received from Hughes and Johnson helped her grow as a poet and writer. One of the most influential Black Newspapers, *The Chicago Defender,* published 75 of Brooks's poems when she was between the ages of 16 and 17 years old: "As with other black writers, [Brooks] will discover the world of books and the joy of imagination while still young. Encouraged by her mother, she will create a world of her own—a world of words" (Towns, 1974, p. 21).

Brooks continued to seek out venues for her writing well into her adulthood. In 1941, Brooks and her husband, Henry Blakeley II who was also a poet and writer, joined a writing workshop held at the South Side Community Art Center organized by Inez Cunningham Stark. At that time, Stark was considered a red-headed "rebel" of sorts by her peers because of her lack of fear going to the "Black Belt" of Chicago to work with "would be Negro poets" (Brooks, 1972, p. 65). Although the workshop was primarily held at the community center, Stark would sometimes have meetings at her home located along the "Gold Coast" of Chicago. According to Brooks, this writing workshop, which included Edward Bland, Margaret Burroughs (Margaret Taylor Goss), John Carlis, William "Bill" Couch, Margaret Cunningham, and Fern Gayden,[3] was the "only" group she experienced "where people really told each other what they thought" (Gayles, 2003, p. 30). In addition to encountering honesty among workshop participants, Brooks underscored that the ability to "bounce the analysis back and forth" among workshop members was an effective pedagogical strategy (p. 60). The South Side Community Art Center writing workshop was the foundation for early drafts of Brooks's *A Street in Bronzeville* (1945) that depicted lives in the kitchenette buildings for Blacks in Chicago:

> My idea was to take my own street and write about a person or incident associated with each of the houses on the block . . . There was not one Negro east of Cottage Grove Avenue . . . The book had a rather folksy narrative nature, and I guess that is one way to get poetry in front of people: to tell stories. Everyone loves stories, and a surprising number of people can be trapped in a book of verse if there's a promise of a story.
>
> (Gayles, 2003, p. 32)

Brooks was an ethnographer in many ways who saw poetry in her neighborhood and among the faces of Black people; she also believed that poets had the responsibility of being able to see and hear more than anyone. For example in "kitchenette building" which is part of *A Street in Bronzeville*, Brooks introduces readers to the "Grayed in, and gray . . ." where "'Dream' makes a giddy sound, not strong/Like 'rent,' 'feeding a wife, 'satisfying a man.'" In later interviews, she tried to explain that her poetry addressed black life in organic ways; in other words she did not intentionally write for or about Black people but since she found inspiration in her community and among Blacks she wrote about them by default. This is especially important because critics have tried to delineate between her work prior to 1967 and after 1967—a year in which she began to identify herself as "Black" and made blackness the core of her writing.

The *Norton Anthology of African-American Literature* edited by Henry Louis Gates Jr. and Nellie Y. McKay (1997) situates Brooks's work in "Realism, Naturalism, Modernism" marking the period between 1940–1960. However, they also assert that Brooks's poetry "defies" this heading. Poet and scholar Elizabeth Alexander contextualizes Brooks's early poetry within "prescribed European" forms which was indicative of Black writers and poets in the first half of the twentieth century: "Brooks's generational predecessors whom we know she read and studied and who, like her, favored the sonnet" (2005, p. xviii). Once again Alexander's observations are important in that she contextualizes Brooks's desire to master the sonnet in a larger trajectory of Black writers following European models of writing and literacy. Brooks's point of departure, according to Alexander, was that she "worked with expert subtlety to make the sonnet her own." As Brooks's poetry told the stories of Chicago's Blackbelt, she crafted these stories within the existing frameworks of the lyric, ballad, and sonnet poem. While Brooks's early work was not a part of a particular renaissance or movement, she and her husband were a part of a community of artists in Chicago who were questioning the world. Brooks recalled that 1941–1949 was the "party era":

> My husband and I knew writers, knew painters, knew pianists and dancers and actresses, knew photographers galore. There were always weekend parties to be attended, where we merry Bronzevillians could find each other and earnestly philosophize sometimes on into the dawn . . . Great social decisions were reached. Great solutions, for great problems, were provided . . . Of course, in that time, it was believed, still, that the society could be prettied, quieted, cradled, *sweetened*, (Brooks's emphasis) if only people talked enough, glared at each other yearningly enough, waited enough.
>
> (1972, p. 68)

Brooks's self-reflection demonstrates her belief during the 1950s and early 1960s that eventually the United States would embrace Black people. Brooks's tactical goal at that time was to wait in hopes that the political and social climate would eventually be "prettied, quieted, cradled, *sweetened*." At this point, her poetry and words were brilliant displays of Black humanity but they were merely waiting and wanting words unfamiliar with the movement that would force them off the page. When Brooks met a "new Black" who also had grown tired of talking and waiting, her poetry and life would be catapulted into an urgent free verse while re-establishing the importance of reading, writing, speaking, and doing the word.

The Second Annual Black Writers' Conference and Post-1967 Discourse

An analysis of post-1967 interviews with Brooks reveals an undeniable shift in her understanding of the role and responsibility of Black writers and work they produced. The story is one of transformation and an awakening that one might expect from a novice writer. However, Brooks's story demonstrates her openness as an established writer to learn from a younger generation who embraced blackness in a bold way that was initially foreign, but appealing, to her. In *Report from Part One*, Brooks reflects on her initial reception at the Black Writers' Conference at Fisk University in Nashville,[4] Tennessee as being "coldly respected" (Brooks, 1972, p. 84). In other words, in the context of this conference Brooks was an established poet-elder with a national reputation. However, her relevance in this time and place was second to the new "heroes" present at this conference. The new heroes, according to Brooks, were not only poets and writers but also playwrights and historians who were committed to Black people in print, in spirit, and in life. Additionally, these new heroes distinguished their movement from the Harlem Renaissance in the 1920s by underscoring their desire to be wholly independent of white sponsorship that they believed compromised Black voices. Brooks noted that although the participants at this conference may not have known it yet, Amiri Baraka was their leader. In this era, Black writers unapologetically focused on the social, political, and economic concerns in Black communities throughout the world in their work. Don L. Lee's (1971a) essay "Toward a Definition: Black Poetry in the Sixties (after LeRoi Jones)" argued that poetry had been an "exclusive" genre and "preferred by the intellectually astute." The problem with this exclusivity, Lee asserted, was "the poetry on the written page very seldom found its way into the home or neighborhood of the common black man" (Lee, 1971b, p. 236). The desire to eradicate notions of class distinctions among Blacks was important to writers and activists of the Black Arts Movement; the more divided Blacks were along class lines, the less likely they were to advance socially and economically.

Although Brooks was raised in a loving home where her passion for writing was cultivated and nurtured, Blackness or Black pride was not an explicit doctrine in her household. Brooks writes of being isolated from her peers because of her dark skin and the fact that she had beautiful clothes made by an aunt who was a seamstress. In the opening sentences to her autobiography *Report from Part One*, Brooks discloses "When I was a child, it did not occur to me, even once, that the black in which I was encased (I called it brown in those days) would be considered, one day, beautiful" (Brooks, 1972, p. 37). While Brooks's pre-1967 poetry was about Black people, there was not a strategic conscious effort to be a part of a Black community of writers who wrote specifically for a Black audience. Lee notes that the poetry and writings of the Black Arts Movement associated with the 1960s was "not too different from Black poetry of the forties and fifties; there has always existed in the verse a certain amount of blackness" (1971a, p. 238). However, Blackness in "verse" as opposed to Blackness in action were two distinct issues. Brooks's poetic portraits of Black life in Chicago found in *A Street in Bronzeville* like the aforementioned "kitchenette building," "the mother," "a song in the front yard," and "the preacher: ruminates behind the sermon" were examples of blackness in verse. However, Brooks decidedly expanded her blackness from her verse to her activism and work with young people. In an interview with Ida Lewis, the editor of *Essence* magazine, in spring 1971, Brooks explained her "turning point":

> The real turning point came in 1967, when I went to the Second Black Writers' Conference at Fisk University. I had been on tour and I was tired and wanted to get home, and I just thought I would whiz through Fisk, give my little reading, and come on back here to Chicago. But I found what has stimulated my life these last three years: young people, full of a new spirit. They seemed stronger and taller, really ready to take on the challenges.
>
> (Brooks, 1972, p. 167)

In her autobiography, Brooks explained that prior to arriving at Fisk University in Nashville, Tennessee, she had a reading at South Dakota State College where the all-white audience "loved" her. Brooks had every intention of doing her reading at Fisk University and moving on quickly and quietly; however, she found herself enthralled by the energy of the young Black writers present: "I had never been before, in the general presence of such insouciance, such live firmness, such confident vigor, such determination to mold or carve something DEFINITE" (Brooks, 1972, p. 85).

According to her autobiography, Brooks attended the conference with Margaret Danner Cunningham and noted that in the context of the

Black Writers' Conference demographics the two of them were "Old Girls" and "Has-beens" (p. 84). The "new black," Brooks duly noted, was a "tall walker" and proud of his or her blackness and institutionalized this pride not only in appearance but in writing, speech, action, as well as establishing Independent Black Institutions. Brooks made herself a student of this "new black" and entered what she referred to as the "kindergarten of consciousness" while substituting her largely white list of writing heroes with writers like Nikki Giovanni, Amiri Baraka and Haki Madhubuti:

> They baptized her whole in deep waters of Black consciousness from which she emerged bearing witness for the empowerment, joy, and peace that comes from knowing self, loving self, and being loved by her people.
>
> (Gayles, 2003, p. xiii)

Responding to questions from Eugenia Collier, George Kent, and Dudley Randall in a 1973 interview, Brooks was asked about her change in form, referencing her once traditional styles of poetry. Brooks, still making sense of her newfound consciousness, discussed the evolution of her work:

> No, I'm not writing sonnets, and I probably won't be, because as I've said many times, this does not seem to be a sonnet time. It seems to be a free verse time, because this is a raw, ragged, uneven time—with rhymes, if there are rhymes, incidental and random . . . I am in transition. I want to reach all manner of black people. That's my urgent compulsion.
>
> (p. 68)

Brooks talked about writing poems that were small enough to fit in her purse so that she could pull them out and read them at a moment's notice. Brooks and others during the Black Arts Movement valued publishing and they also sought to make their writing accessible to non-readers. Poems were published in small and manageable anthologies or broadsides that could be carried in pockets and purses. Much of her inspiration for this urgency was inspired by her relationship with fellow Chicagoan Don L. Lee. Together with other poets, Lee and Brooks would recite their work in unlikely venues like bars and taverns in an attempt to take poetry to the Black people who may not have attended poetry readings or political rallies. This gesture embodied the spirit of the Black Arts Movement and the way African American literate practices have been reinvented throughout history. Recall, I discuss Brown's analysis of Black writing serving as a "call;" that is, anything written is done so with the intention that it will be spoken and serve as a rallying cry. This understanding of the role of poetry and prose did not negate the need for the printed word; poets and writers of the Black Arts Movement were extremely committed to publishing their work. However, in addition to writing, the poets in this movement liberated words from the physical page to demonstrate the continuum of written and spoken words. In an interview with *Black Books Bulletin*, Brooks responded to a question about her reason for writing. She described her writing trajectory as having three distinct "departments." The first being the positive things in her environment, "Dandelions and clouds, love and enemies, friends" (*Black Books Bulletin*, 1974, p. 29). In the second department, Brooks experienced integration in Hyde Park High School in Chicago which was mostly white. Brooks explained, "I began to sense that if we screamed loudly enough and showed how truly wonderful we were, that sooner or later Whites would open up their arms and embrace us and invite us to share the feast." This perspective, of course embodied the premature hope of integration—a hope that the Black Power and Black Arts Movement participants believed was never fully realized. In the third department of her writing development Brooks contended that young poets like Don L. Lee influenced her to see Black poetry differently:

> I began to understand that Black Afrikans should be concerned about Blackness. And I believe that with Don and other young writers, that Black poetry is written by Blacks, about Blacks, to Blacks. That is where I am now and expect to stay.
>
> (*Black Books Bulletin*, 1974, p. 30)

Not only did Brooks incorporate this philosophy of writing for Blacks into her writing, she also took this ideology into her literacy activism with young people through her teaching, mentoring, and organizing of writing workshops and programs.

A Pedagogy of Possibility

The Second Annual Black Writers' Conference in 1967 at Fisk University obviously was not the sole catalyst for Brooks's literacy activism. Poet, jazz musician, and activist, Oscar Brown Jr. sent a telegram to Brooks inviting her to a production he directed called *Opportunity Please Knock* starring members of the Blackstone Rangers. The Rangers, a notorious Chicago gang, in many ways represented the great heartache of the northern migration for hopeful Black families.[5] Once in Chicago, as Brooks has documented in her poetry, black families found themselves frequently out of work and living in deplorable conditions. Seeking refuge in gangs was only one of the pitfalls of struggling Black youth. Artists like Oscar Brown Jr. saw the potential of the young people in the Blackstone Rangers and created a production that showcased their multiple talents. For Brown, "the lines between the respectable and disreputable, the aspiring middle class and the so-called underclass, were never assumed ... to be absolute" (Saul, 2003, p. 93). Brown's worldview was demonstrated in *Opportunity Please Knock* which was a collaboration between the Blackstone Rangers and students from Malcolm X College. Together, these two groups of young people worked on Brown's musical "Slave Song" as well as "Great Nitty Gritty." Brown and Brooks shared the belief that young people, regardless of class and social status, could use writing and performance as a way to confront violence, poverty, and possibly think about a new way of living. Later, Martin Luther King Jr. would share his reflection of the potential of members of the Blackstone Rangers who marched with him in Chicago exercising nonviolent discipline.[6] Brooks has retold the story of seeing *Opportunity Please Knock* many times but the core remains the same; Brooks immediately wanted to extend her resources to members of the Blackstone Rangers. This would be one of many ways that Brooks began to reach out to Black youth. Brooks believed that she was most useful meeting people where they were, even if that meant gangs, prisons, and other out-of-school contexts. Brooks described her understanding of the responsibility of Black poets to work with youth in an interview with Paul Angle at her home in 1967:

> Let us *take* art to those who are not going to get it otherwise. I believe, for instance, creative writing workshops for the very many interested young would be rewarding. I am working in this

way now through Oscar Brown's Alley Theatre projects on the South Side of Chicago, and the talent I find is exciting, the eagerness inspiring.

(Brooks, 1972, p. 142)

Taking art to the unexpected places was part of the Black Arts Movement blueprint. In addition to writers, jazz musicians, as well as other artists, were invested in self-reliance and self-determination while challenging traditional ideas about where teaching and learning could take place. They also challenged who was considered a teacher. Literacy research that examines out-of-school contexts does not always acknowledge the contributions these movements made for the way education is conceptualized beyond the classroom. The writing workshop that Brooks orchestrated for the Blackstone Rangers began at the First Presbyterian Church for the first 6–8 months. Initially there were 20 participants. Brooks was careful not to refer to herself as a "teacher" or to her practices as "teaching." However, Brooks did consider herself a "friend" to workshop participants:

They made it plain that they did not want me to "teach" them anything about the sonnet form or such . . . But, as I say, we were friends that talked about our poetry and read our poetry to each other. And also talked about what was going on in society. They taught me many things I had not known before.

(*Black Books Bulletin*, 1974, p. 30)

The original workshop not only included members from the Rangers but also the "older young" which included Don L. Lee (Haki Madhubuti); Alicia Johnson, Jim Taylor, Mike Cook, and Peggy Susberry. There was the "one high schooler," Sharon Scott, as well as Walter Bradford, Carl Clark, Jim Cunningham, Jewel Latimore (Johari Amini), Carolyn Rodgers, Doris Turner, and Sigmonde Wimberli. After Brooks saw that Bradford was an ideal "teenage organizer," she asked him to continue to lead the workshop while she financed it by purchasing dictionaries, books, and magazines for one year. Brooks's principled decision to ask Walter Bradford, a younger poet who had successfully worked with teens who found themselves in gangs, demonstrated her understanding that this work had to be an intergenerational effort:

I don't believe that such groups should be masterminded by their adult initiators indefinitely, and I'm assisting one of the young men in the group to take over my "duties" when a year has passed I would like him to emphasize, especially, involving some of the very able members of the South Side teen gangs.

(Brooks, 1972, p. 142)

Brooks admittedly believed Bradford would make a stronger leader for the workshop over time. Brooks never took her role for granted—"Adult initiators," according to Brooks, were just that. The eventual goal, demonstrated by Brooks's desire to move out of the way, was for other young people to develop leadership skills and continue the work in interesting and innovative ways.

Brooks's poem, "The Blackstone Rangers," captures the young men and women in three parts from three different perspectives. In Part I of her poem, "AS SEEN BY DISCIPLINES," Brooks describes these young men using an outsider lens:

There they are.
Thirty at the corner.
Black, raw, ready.
Sores in the city
that do not want to heal.

Brooks transports readers to corners that could have been found in any urban city in the United States. The rawness represented both these young men's vulnerability and their tipping point. These "sores in the city" may have been unsightly for passers-by but the Rangers learned to accept their positionality. This poem was part of Brooks's book *In the Mecca* (1964) which has two sections, "In the Mecca" and "After Mecca." The former, referred to as Brooks's "epic of Black humanity" (Lee, 1972, p. 22). "In the Mecca" takes readers on a complicated journey with a mother who is looking for her missing daughter, Pepita, in the maze of her apartment building only to discover that the young girl has been murdered. Pepita was a young poet and the "hope of her family and community" (Alexander, 2005, p. xxiii). The Mecca, an apartment building that was once home to wealthy whites, and later inhabited by elite Blacks, evolved into a notoriously volatile living space for Chicago's Black and poor. At 19 years old, Brooks worked as a secretary for a healer named "Dr. French" whose office was located in the Mecca; her experiences working for French informed some of her poem and "The Blackstone Rangers" appears in the second part of the book. In a study of women poets in the Black Arts Movement entitled *After Mecca*, Clarke argues that "In the Mecca" is Brooks's effort to honor "the sacred and vexed places of language, literature, and poetry within the culture of Black America" (Clarke, 2006, p. 27). Brooks placed the Rangers in the maze of uncertainty the Mecca created as well as the saturation of poverty and violence in a concentrated area. In the second part of the poem entitled "The Leaders," Brooks speaks to a new sense of Black Nationalism that was being aroused in the hearts, minds, and attitudes of many black people while the Rangers maintained their own leaders and thus their own "Nation":

> Jeff, Gene, Geronimo. And Bop.
> They cancel, cure and curry.
> Hardly the dupes of the downtown thing
> The cold bonbon,
> The rhinestone thing. And hardly in a hurry.
> Hardly Belafonte, King,
> Black Jesus, Stokely, Malcolm X or Rap.
> Bungled trophies.
> Their country is a Nation on no map.

Brooks's poem shows the leaders of the Rangers as having a system and rituals even though they are not understood or acknowledged outside of their own institution. Brooks also notes that the leaders are "hardly" the voices of the Civil Rights and Black Power Movements, [Harry] Belafonte, [Martin Luther] King, Stokely [Carmichael], Malcolm X, or [H.] Rap [Brown]. Belafonte, a singer and actor, wholeheartedly used his influence to support the Civil Rights Movement while Stokely Carmichael, and H. Rap Brown as well as their ideological predecessor Malcolm X were focused on "Black Power." Here, the young Rangers were depicted as being on the periphery of these movements while living in a country within a country. There was a movement all around them of which they were oblivious because they were engaged in their own struggles. However, the "nation" occupied by the Rangers is further removed as "Their country" is "on no map."

One of the essential practices in the workshop Brooks started for the Blackstone Rangers—and one she used throughout her work with fellow poets—was for her to be a "friend" to fellow writers. In an interview with Claudia Tate (1983), Brooks made it clear that the Rangers did not necessarily understand who she was, "[The Rangers] didn't know what in the world I was about. And why should they? But we worked" (Tate, 1983, pp. 40–41). Brooks did not expect or anticipate that these young gang members would immediately embrace her or understand her; Brooks's purpose was to provide a space and an opportunity for them to work side by side. This method was ideologically intertwined with Brooks's belief that the best teachers of writing were indeed writers themselves. Brooks listened to participants and invited their vision to help create the format for these workshops. Brooks was also committed to reintroducing poetry to young people who developed distaste for all things poetic in their school experiences:

> The people in the workshops have told me, over and over again, that they had hated poetry because they were forced to memorize it in elementary school and high school, and it was presented to them as something heavy, to be gotten through for the sake of grades.
>
> (Gayles, 2003, p. 34)

All too often Brooks heard from young writers and potential poets that poetry in schools had in many ways become standardized and reduced to recitation and grading. Brooks's pedagogy of possibility invited students to be creative and use their writing for personal liberation:

> The thing I am interested in doing is in presenting poetry as a living thing, an instrument of pleasure, of release, and [students] enjoy it when it's given to them that way. I make them write a lot and once in a while they'll groan about that. Each student must write a book of twenty or twenty-five poems, depending upon the time we have . . . My motto could be: "It's all in the doing."
>
> (Gayles, 2003, p. 34)

Brooks did not ask students to do anything she was not doing herself. Elsewhere, I have examined the lives of teacher poets and poet elders who are "practitioners of the craft" (Fisher, 2005a, 2005b, 2007b). In sum, practitioners of the craft teach by doing or engaging in the practices they are promoting; students or learners learn by seeing their elders take risks in their writing and exposing their own vulnerability that can manifest during the composing process. As a practitioner of the craft, Brooks sought to give her students the work ethic of a writer who was not bound by grades. Brooks also brought established writers like James Baldwin and John Oliver Killens to the young writers with whom she worked. Her understanding of the need for her to become a "friend" to young writers illustrated the importance of building relationships of trust and respect in a writing community. Relative to her young Black writers, Brooks's discoveries are consistent with both historical and contemporary interpretations of literacy learning. Such learning is at once communal and participatory for people of African descent and is a key point that was emphasized in the previous chapter (Perry, 2003). Additionally, her desire to portray poetry as a "living thing" required experiencing writing as an organic process. Brooks's work with young writers transformed her pedagogy of possibility to a hands-on reality.

One of the projects that emerged from Brooks's workshops was *Jump Bad: A New Chicago Anthology* (1971). Brooks considered this anthology to be the most significant accomplishment of the workshop. She was also proud that the workshop opened its doors to singers, dancers, and other performance artists in addition to poets and writers. *Jump Bad*, published by Dudley Randall's Black-owned and operated Broadside Press—a strategically chosen press, as I will show—was dedicated to Hoyt Fuller who was described as a "Great Editor-Warm Educator." Brooks was particularly candid about the influence the workshop participants, or the "Jump Badders," had on her personally:

> With the arrival of these people my neatly-paced life altered almost with a jerk. Never did they tell me to "change" my hair to "natural." But soon I did. Never did they tell me to open my eyes, to look about me. But soon I did. Never did they tell me to find them sane, serious, substantial, superseding. But soon I did.
>
> (Brooks, 1971, p. 12)

Brooks, referencing her once straightened hair (later celebrated in her poem "To Those of My Sisters Who Kept Their Naturals"), allowed herself to be inspired by the increasing consciousness of young Blacks which included embracing "Blackness." As the United States and the Caribbean were experiencing the Black Arts Movement, Chicago had its own wing (Crawford, 2006). A cultural production of the Chicago Black Arts Movement existed on a wall on the corner of 43rd and Langley. The mural, called "The Wall of Respect" and completed the same year Brooks experienced a shift in her poet identity, included figures like Malcolm X, Stokely Carmichael, and Marcus Garvey. A jazz and blues section of the mural featured a striking presentation of the singer Billie Holiday. Murals were the people's billboards that informed, educated while exuding pride. Brooks, too, was included in this visual representation of Blacks who were forging new paths for others (Figure 2.1). These young poets inspired Brooks to continue to write about black lives as she did in her earlier writing but with more deliberateness. They encouraged Brooks to not only serve as an ethnographer of Black lives and experiences but to also be prepared to use her writing to critique injustices and incite action. In the introduction to *Jump Bad*, Brooks addressed her role in the workshop with great humility and humor:

> Incidentally, the question of my status, my position, (was I or was I not a Teacher, a Workshop Ruler?) was soon a gentle joke.

Figure 2.1 "Gwendolyn Brooks and the Wall of Respect" by Bob Crawford.

I "taught" nothing. I told them, almost timidly, what I knew, what I had learned from European models (well, Langston Hughes too!) And they told me without telling me that the European "thing" was not what they were about.

(1971, p. 12)

Brooks addressed her natural inclination to show these young people devices and forms consistent with what she learned coming of age in the 1940s and 1950s. Brooks and her peers were educated to believe that the sonnet and other European forms were the norm. The "European thing" lost its ground during the Black Arts Movement because many young artists were aching to see their own images in art and hear their own voices as well as those of the people they knew and loved. To return to an earlier observation made by Madhubuti, poetry in the 1960s demanded relevance to the everyday person. Editing anthologies was another form of institution-building; it would allow future generations to experience the writing of a community of voices on the periphery of the canon. Following the Jump Badders' charge, she changed her approach rather than asking them to change theirs:

Eventually I gave up imposing exercises—and we became friends. We discussed Issues [Brooks's capitalization], we read our work to each other, sometimes criticizing, sometimes not. We respected and liked each other, in spite of occasional attitude clashes. The first and unifying thing we understood about each other was that we were, all of us, Black . . . The second thing we recognized was that we all most anxiously "wanted to write."

(p. 12)

As Brooks provided opportunities for young black poets and writers to polish their craft, exchange feedback, and publish, she continued to open herself to learning as much as she could from them as well. Brooks's intentions were to become a relevant poet by crafting poems that were accessible to all Black people, reading more widely, supporting Independent Black Institutions and providing scholarships and writing competitions for emerging writers in urban public schools in Chicago. Brooks and her younger protégés, South African poet Keorapetse Kgositsile, Haki Madhubuti, and Dudley Randall, collaborated on a blueprint for writing Black poetry. In this "capsule course," published by

Dudley Randall's Broadside Press, Brooks gave an overview of the new directions for Black writing:

> The new black ideal italicizes black identity, black solidarity, black self-possession and self-address. The new black literature subscribes to these. Furthermore, the *essential* black ideal vitally acknowledges African roots. To those roots the new black literature cooperatively subscribes. The prevailing understanding: black literature is literature BY blacks, ABOUT blacks, directed TO blacks. ESSENTIAL black literature is the distillation of black life.
>
> (Brooks, 1975a, p. 3)

Brooks's pre-1967 poetry always presented the "distillation of Black life." The major difference between pre- and post-1967 discourses was that her promotion of Blackness became more pronounced during the "years of explosion" (p. 3). Brooks argued that between 1966–1968, Black poets and writers were trading in Shakespeare and T.S. Eliot for Frantz Fanon's *The Wretched of the Earth* and Malcolm X's *The Autobiography of Malcolm X* as well as the rhythms of jazz musicians. Brooks, whose early writing was influenced by Shakespeare, Wordsworth, Tennyson, and Shelley or who she once referred to as "the conventional loves of youth" (Gayle, 2003, p. 4) began to understand the emergence of the new "classics." *The Autobiography of Malcolm X* and writings by Frantz Fanon forged a new path for essential reading for Black people.[7] With the encouragement of her younger colleagues who she affectionately referred to as her "sons of revolution" (p. 112), Brooks forged a new canon that also included W.E.B. DuBois's *The Souls of Black Folk* and anything by Zora Neale Hurston. Brooks had also been encouraged to read Ferdinand Lundberg's *The Rich and the Super Rich*. This new canon inspired Brooks to reconsider writing poetry specifically for Black people. In addition to contextualizing the need for such a volume specifically addressing the how-tos of Black poetry writing, Brooks and her co-authors offered their own individual advice. Brooks generated a list of eight "hints" which included using everyday language or "ordinary speech" in writing. Brooks also emphasized the need to choose words carefully and wisely by asserting "every word must work." Lastly, Brooks advised writers to "loosen" their "rhythms" in order to free their writing to reflect humanity (pp. 10–11). Brooks's post-1967 discourse was at once instructive yet self-reflective of her personal growth and development. She remained humble and aware that she was a work in progress:

> Lessons for myself and thee! For I am a poet with much to learn about what will make poems work for all my people. I am learning slowly. The self education is a poem-by-poem, almost a line-by-line process—with many a reverse, many a lapse.
>
> (Brooks, 1975b, p. 18)

Embracing her own "lapses" in her process of "self-education," Brooks did her best to demystify and to make the process of poetry writing as transparent as possible for writers. Brooks underscored that even she—a Pulitzer Prize-winning poet with endless honors and awards—was still learning and retooling. Brooks's pedagogy of possibility was also evident in her work in prisons. As she redefined her purpose as a poet to make her writing relevant and accessible to all Black people whoever and wherever they may have been, Brooks was also clear about the need for outreach in prisons:

> And of course, I have to be very careful about including prisoners because some of our best work is coming from prisons. Where people are at last having time to sit down and think over their lives and then to reflect, meditate and develop their thoughts in poetry and exciting fiction.
>
> (*Black Books Bulletin*, 1974, p. 32)

Brooks worked with inmates in Stormville, New York, at the Greenhaven Correctional Facility in which inmates served as judges in a poetry contest. Brooks also mentored poet Etheridge Knight during his incarceration. Knight, author of *Poems from Prison* (1968), was serving an eight-year sentence in Indiana State Prison when he began to correspond and develop a relationship with Brooks and Randall who published his collection with Broadside Press. In the short and poetic preface to *Poems from Prison*, Brooks wrote, "Vital. Vital. This poetry is a major announcement," which in many ways summoned Baraka's "S.O.S." (Brooks, 1968). In Knight's poem, "The Sun Came," he begins with borrowed words from Brooks's poem/tribute to Malcolm X: "And if sun comes/How shall we greet him?" Using the sun as a metaphor for Malcolm X, Knight asserts, "The sun came, Miss Brooks . . . He came spitting fire from his lips." Ultimately, Knight and many other activists concurred that Black people did not listen or adhere to Malcolm X's words when he was alive but saw the truth of his teaching after his death. Upon his release, Knight joined fellow poets in the Black Arts Movement and continued to write and publish. Most importantly, he continued to learn and began to teach. During the movement, Black writers and activists gave careful consideration to Black prisoners with hopes to help the incarcerated embrace writing, reading, and speaking out as a method for healing and transforming their lives. Formerly incarcerated men and women, like Knight, had a seat waiting for them at the table if they were committed to using their gifts and talents in a productive way.

Brooks's role as a writing mentor has been largely documented in her relationship with Haki Madhubuti. In his preface to Brooks's auto-biography, "Gwendolyn Brooks: Beyond the Wordmaker—The making of an African Poet," Madhubuti writes:

> Gwendolyn Brooks' post-1967 poetry is fat-less. Her new work resembles a man getting off meat, turning to a vegetarian diet. What one immediately notices is that all the excess weight is quickly lost.
>
> (p. 22)

Brooks wrote alongside her students and for her students; this is most evident in her post-1967 writings. In her poem, "Young Afrikans," Brooks pays tribute to the new poets who "jerk" the new day "out of joint," and hence, demonstrating her new style and commitment to young writers. "Young Afrikans" also demonstrates Brooks's efforts to embrace a Pan-African ideology:

> Young Africans
>   of the furious
> Who take Today and jerk it out of joint
> have made new underpinnings and a head
>
> Blacktime is wonderful for chimeful
> poemhood
> but they decree a
> Jagged chiming now.
>
> If there are flowers flowers
> Must come out to the road. Rowdy!—
> knowing where wheels and people are,

knowing where whips and screams are,
knowing where deaths are, where the kind kills are.

As for that other kind of kindness,
if there is milk it must be mindful,
The milkofhumankindess must be mindful
as wily wines.
Must be fine fury.
Must be mega, must be main.

Taking Today (to jerk it out of joint)
the hardheroic maim the
leechlike-as-usual who use,
adhere to, carp, and harm.

And they await,
across the Changes and the spiraling dead,
our black revival, our black vinegar,
our hands, and our hot blood.
                    (Reprinted by Consent of Brooks Permissions)

Consistent with her accounts of how her life was radically changed by a younger generation of poets and writers, Brooks captured the urgency of Black poetry writing. "Blacktime," or the era of self-reliance and self-love sounded a call for "poemhood." The flowers that Brooks speaks of in her poem are far from the symbols of nature and harmony in the poetry of her youth. These "flowers" are cognizant of the screams that follow untimely deaths of Black youth and leaders. Brooks brought her work even closer to home with youth in her neighborhood. In the early 1970s, Brooks decided to organize the young people on her block for a summer reading and writing group. Brooks continued to live in Chicago's South Side throughout her lifetime. Initially, Brooks wanted to "corral" about 30 children; however, she was able to organize and work with 18 high school students over a four-year time period.[8] This collective of high school students, T.H.E.M (Trying Hard to Express Myself), met at Brooks's home to discuss a range of topics including "school, sex, drugs, politics, and Africa" (Gayles, 2003, p. 115). Brooks's main objective was to expose students to many types of writers and provide opportunities for them to experience life beyond their block:

I wanted to help extend the horizons of these young people, and they met with me for about four years. During that time I gave them scholarships, took them to black plays and movies, bought books and educational magazines for them, brought "career people" to speak to them—writers, a senator, a photographer, and editor, an actress. They were not shy in the presence of these career people: they challenged, corrected, extended. (These youngsters were also "watchworkers," who kept a collective eye on the block and reported disturbances to the police.) Our best-enjoyed nourishment, however, was the unrestricted exhilaration of "mere" communication.

(Gayles, 2003, p. 115)

One student proclaimed that she did not understand what she, a young Black girl in Chicago, Illinois, had to do with Africa. Brooks responded by sending the young woman on a trip to Ghana, West Africa. Brooks's daughter, Nora Brooks Blakely, served as the student's chaperone. Brooks was careful not to portray herself or anyone else as having the power to "give" young poets a "voice." She did, however, encourage young poets to use what she believed they already possessed (see Gayles, pp. 19–20). In her poem, "Speech To The Young. Speech To The Progress-Toward (Among them Nora and Henry III)," Brooks instructs young people to continue to be engaged in struggle rather than seeking comfort in the progress that has preceded them:

Say to them,
say to the down-keepers,
the sun-slappers,
the self-soilers,
the harmony-hushers,
"Even if you are not ready for day
it cannot always be night."
You will be right
For that is the hard home-run.

Live not for battles won.
Live not for the end-of-the-song.
Live in the along.

(Reprinted by Consent of Brooks Permissions)

The ideology that permeated the movements of the 1960s and 1970s sought to replace the "down-keepers," "sun-slappers," "self-soilers," and "harmony-hushers" with literacy advocates and activists. These advocates and activists sincerely believed in Black youth and Independent Black Institutions that promoted the re-education of Black people. Literacy advocates and activists continued the Black quest for education, literacy, and economic independence. Brooks's literacy activism is not a lesson in history; her life and work are a blueprint for the now as evidenced in the final chapter of this work. Her willingness to open herself to the lives of younger generations when she could have walked away with her titles demonstrates how Black poets and writers have used their writing to organize and mobilize. Brooks's political move from Harper and Row to Dudley Randall's Broadside Press in 1969 and eventually to Haki Madhubuti's Third World Press further demonstrated her desire to support Independent Black Institutions (IBIs). The "initial spark" for Broadside Press was Randall's printing of his poem "Ballad of Birmingham" which was a response to the bombing of Sixteenth Street Baptist Church on September 15, 1963, in Birmingham, Alabama (Thompson, 1999, p. 28). Randall, who also wanted to "bring poetry back to the people" and "give people joy" funded his publishing company by using his first paycheck from his work as a librarian. Poets like Madhubuti, Sonia Sanchez, Etheridge Knight, Carolyn Rodgers, Jayne Cortez, Audre Lorde, Addison Gayle Jr., Margaret Walker and many more published with Randall's Broadside Press. When Randall met Brooks in 1966 he had been an admirer of her writing and read about her in Hoyt Fuller's *Negro Digest*. Brooks not only told Randall he could use any of her poems for a broadside but insisted that she publish her autobiography, *Report from Part One*, with his company. In a study of Randall's Broadside Press, Boyd (2003) asserts that Randall was honest with Brooks about the possibility of her losing money by leaving Harper and Row. However, the fear of losing money was not enough to deter Brooks:

> Brooks not only changed her publisher, she changed her vocabulary. Under the influence of the younger writers, she began writing in a style more in sync with a black-consciousness audience. As an institution builder, she gave her reputation, her poetry, her skill, and her home in the service of the cultural struggle.
>
> (Boyd, p. 168)

Madhubuti reminded readers in the first installment of Brooks's autobiography that her purposeful move to Independent Black Institutions made her "the *doer* and not just the sayer"[9] (Lee, p. 25). Brooks became a "doer" by not only moving her work to Black publishing houses but also becoming a board member for Don L. Lee's Institute for Positive Education (IPE) in Chicago which included Third World Press, New Concept Development Center (NCDC), and a publication devoted to Black literature called *Black Books Bulletin*. Brooks made contributions to *Black Books Bulletin* and was even the primary focus of one of the issues. This metaphorical "bulletin" for Black writers, readers and publishers featured a "continuing" bibliography of books published by Black presses and about Black people globally. Lee, the first editor of the journal, explained that the aim of the publication was to provide information to the many mentors in the Black community:

> In our small way, THE BLACK BOOKS BULLETIN will try to supply positive information and images to black people who influence other black people, such as teachers (elementary, high school, college, etc.), postal workers, policemen, librarians, students, doctors, lawyers, dentists, nurses, writers, artists and others. It is premature to think that we can reach the masses of black people . . . but we do feel that we can reach some of the people who influence and direct the lives of others.
>
> (Lee, 1971b, p. 25)

Not only was *Black Books Bulletin* concerned with reaching "formal" educators but also men and women who were potential mentors to Black people through everyday interactions with social services and other leadership fields. At the core of this mission statement was the belief that teaching and learning occurred daily and that literacy learning was important for Black people. During this time, there was a movement to create schools where these values and beliefs would be infused directly into the curriculum. Brooks thrust herself into the culture of institution building.

Chapter 2 demonstrated how Brooks's life and work exemplify the movement toward institution-building and how Brooks and others in the Black Arts Movement sought to recreate the communal values in literacy. Brooks's body of work and activism illustrate several important pieces in the development of Black literate lives. Brooks revisits the need for building IBIs such as Black publishing houses as well as organizing collectives of young writers. Brooks not only stops preaching to the choir so to speak or sharing her work in the expected places, but returns poetry to the everyday person. She demands that her words inspire in all contexts and settings in hopes to engage the man or woman who became dismayed by the way poetry and writing had been reduced to grades in schools. From the college students, to the prisoner, to the undiscovered poet, Brooks paved a road to create relevant teaching and learning communities that met young people where they were. Brooks accomplished this by bringing her writing to life through dialogue, public readings, and oral exchanges in collectives and workshops in living rooms, churches, community centers, and campuses.

While Brooks was engaged in this struggle primarily in Chicago, the sirens of necessity were sounding throughout the United States. The same poets, writers and artists who fueled the Black Arts Movements and the creation of independent printing presses and journals were also advocates for the education of Black children. "Doers" rather than "sayers" engaged in literate practices and activities beyond poetry. It should be noted, however, that "one could be a prominent 'cultural' nationalist leader without being a poet" (Austin, 2006, p. 95). In the next chapter, I will examine the role of Independent Black Institutions, particularly *Black News* newspaper co-founded by teacher and community activist Jitu Weusi. *Black News*, a publication of the EAST in Brooklyn, New York City, sought to create literate traditions that aimed not only to educate but also to develop self-sustaining Black communities.

CHAPTER 3

Agitating, Educating, and Organizing

The Making of Revolutionary Literacies

In his article "Ocean Hill-Brownsville Revisited: 1969," Leslie Campbell began with a prelude to his critique of the *"business as usual"* atmosphere in the streets of Brooklyn only one year after Black and Puerto Rican students, parents, and teachers demanded community control of neighborhood schools:

> The streets of Ocean Hill-Brownsville are now silent. The shock waves it reeled from in the Fall of 1968 have now subsided. The volcano that spewed forth hot lava is once again sleeping. The hurricane watch has ended and it is now *business as usual.*
>
> (Campbell, *Black News,* October 1969, pp. 1–2)

Campbell's article, appearing on the front page of the second issue of *Black News* newspaper, set the expectation that the readership should still be actively engaged in the struggle for the education of Black youth (Figure 3.1).

The "volcano" Campbell referred to was also known as the "the experiment" to decentralize certain school districts and create local boards to make economic and staffing decisions. Like Chicago's South Side in which Brooks lived and worked, Ocean Hill-Brownsville was an impoverished section of Brooklyn that was predominately Black.

Figure 3.1 Sample cover of *Black News.*

"Community control"[1] and "decentralization" became terms that framed one of New York City's most defining clashes between Blacks and whites once Ocean Hill-Brownville was declared an experimental district (Gordon, 2001; Podair, 2002). With a mostly Black student body and largely white teaching staff and administration, Black youth and their parents were becoming increasingly wary of the curriculum and pedagogical practices employed by the public schools. Like Brooks, young people yearned to have images of themselves. The man who was named the Ocean Hill-Brownsville district unit administrator during the experiment, Rhody McCoy, noted "that most white teachers in New York ... didn't believe in the ability of a black child to learn just as well as a white one" (Podair, 2002, p. 4). New York City's United Federation of Teachers (U.F.T) under the leadership of Fred Nauman and Albert Shanker, the U.F.T. New York City chapter chair and the president respectively, were not only resistant to community control but intervened on behalf of the teachers union. These two men, who considered themselves supporters of the Civil Rights Movement and admirers of Dr. Martin Luther King Jr., put pressure on the city and state officials to block McCoy's efforts to fire teachers who he deemed as hostile to the paradigm shift. The racial and cultural politics in New York City that lurked behind the push for community control came to fruition through a series of confrontations, strikes, and stand-offs. In his study *The strike that changed New York: Blacks, whites and the Ocean Hill-Brownsville crisis*, Podair asserts "At Ocean Hill-Brownsville Blacks punished white New Yorkers for assuming they believed in the same things and for attempting to do their thinking for them" (2002, p. 6).

On the opposing side of the U.F.T. was the African American Teachers Association (A.T.A.) led by Albert Vann. A.T.A. not only supported community control but challenged the ideologically-biased knowledge and the "U.F.T-endorsed treatment that sought to locate blacks within the historical trajectories of white immigrants" (p. 7). Teachers like the aforementioned Les Campbell were infusing African American history, literature, orature, and culture into the curriculum in spite of the U.F.T. backlash. One of the priorities for the A.T.A was to include a "Black curriculum" in the public schools. Preston Wilcox, a theoretician of community control and then an adjunct professor at Columbia University's School of Social work, outlined this curriculum in his report "Control of schools within the black community":

> The Black curriculum proceeds from the position that the Black child is human and educable, with creative capabilities and potential, a desire to contribute to Black nationhood and with a need to incorporate an ability to think for himself ... The student learns as a member of a group, not solely as an individual. Each student is unique and a member of a group.
>
> (Wilcox, 1968)

In addition to the proposed curriculum was a specific philosophy of teaching and learning. Much like the philosophical underpinnings that framed the Black struggle for literacy throughout enslavement, Reconstruction, and the thrust for Black Power and Black Arts Movements, the A.T.A. valued "mutuality, cooperation and community" which were the antitheses of the "middle class New York values of individualism, competition, and materialism" (Podair, 2002, p. 7). And while there are varying perspectives of what happened during this tumultuous time in American public school history, the fact remains that Black children were still being underserved and undereducated.[2] Thus, Campbell's critique of the "business as usual" atmosphere became a precursor to a movement to build Independent Black Institutions (IBIs) that he and others joined in the Ocean Hill-Brownsville aftermath. Campbell's tactical goal was to institute a community newspaper that would remind Black parents and teachers that there was still more work to be done. This community newspaper, *Black News*, would preserve the legacy of Black parents in Ocean Hill-Brownsville and wake the sleeping volcano. *Black News* was not meant to be read and discarded but read, discussed and ultimately used to propel Black youth, parents, and educators to act. The newspaper's mission was provocative—to "agitate, educate, and organize" Black people in New York City, throughout the United States, and eventually the larger African Diaspora.

The aim of this chapter is to examine the efforts *Black News* and how this institution sought to create dialogue in print that would move its readers to become involved in social change in their neighborhoods. *Black News* specifically addressed issues of "mis-education" among Black and Puerto Rican youth in public schools while challenging these schools to create a curriculum that was relevant to the youth they served. It also facilitated a process of "re-education" for Black parents, and educators in the wake of Ocean Hill-Brownsville. *Black News* was part of the EAST, "a cultural and educational center for people of African descent," that not only housed *Black News* but also a food cooperative, a restaurant, and the influential Uhuru Sasa School. Ultimately with the EAST as its umbrella institution, *Black News* championed new and revolutionary literacies for its readership with its efforts to inculcate Black youth and their families with the values of literacy, education, integrity and self-reliance through a "proper" or "correct" Black education. To be literate in the context of *Black News* and the EAST included educational, historical, political and

Black cultural literacies as well as knowledge of music (specifically jazz), theatre and nutrition. Like the post-1967 discourse of Gwendolyn Brooks discussed in the previous chapter, *Black News* aimed to reach all Black people regardless of their educational or socio-economic background. Independent Black Institutions (IBIs) like *Black News* and the EAST provide a critical intersection for understanding Black literate lives because of their efforts to create a movement that underscored the need to develop literate communities as a sustaining force to empower youth and their families.

Creating a "Tell it like it is" Culture: The emergence of *Black News*

The rise of the Black Press is often placed between 1880–1910 (Franklin, 1984). According to Franklin, "literacy and education" were the "major objectives" for these institutions that "signaled the institutionalization of several of the emerging cultural values and beliefs of the Afro American nation" (p. 176). Newspapers, like secret schools, literary societies, and writing groups, were essential institutions for Black people and has been viewed by historians of African American literate practices as "an institution that connects people by articulating the sameness of purpose" (Peterson, 1995, p. 11). The first issue of *Black News* was published in October 1969 and introduced the paper as a "new community publication formed in order to encourage a new involvement and awareness among our people." Although the issue was only 8 pages and sold for ten cents, the staff printed 5,000 copies and they were sold out within a week.[3] In this premier issue, the *Black News* staff argued that Black people could not "afford to have an In Crowd." To be sure, this introductory paragraph on the front cover underscored that not only should the "young militant" read *Black News* but maintained "Grandma should be able to give her rap on Huey [Newton]." In other words, *Black News* sought to minimize the notion of a generation gap among Blacks and argued that it was equally important for the elders and youth to be informed about educational and political struggles locally, nationally, and abroad. The presence of an "In Crowd," according to the editorial staff, would further polarize men and women in Black communities that were already fragile. *Black News* wanted Blacks of all ages and at all socio-economic levels to be engaged in dialogue and active struggle for improving education, housing and politics. This was evidenced by its forthright mission statement: "Our main concern is to agitate, educate, organize. If we don't do these things, we aint' doin nothing!" ("Black News of Bedford Stuyvesant," 1969, p. 1).

In later publications of the EAST, *Black News* was described as being "born in September 1969 out of the frustrations of NO COMMUNICATION among the slaves of our community" (*Outline for a New African Educational Institution: The Uhuru Sasa School Program*, p. 10). Here, the editorial staff compared current conditions in Brooklyn, New York, to those of enslaved Africans; Blacks had formed "tribes" in their various boroughs, neighborhoods, blocks, and buildings, but were not communicating in any systematic way. According to Jitu Weusi, formerly Les Campbell,[4] who was a member of the African American Teachers Association, headmaster of the Uhuru Sasa School and columnist for *Black News*:

> It was early fall 1969—no really, June 1969. We had a meeting at my apartment with 15 people. Serious people . . . We did not have any kind of serious communication organ. Black news-papers at that time were in the hands of Negroes who were always worried about what white people were going to say about us rather than us communicating to us. Especially after Ocean Hill-Brownsville, we needed a paper.
>
> (Jitu Weusi, interview, March 21, 2007)

Weusi believed that Blacks had lost some of their passion after the Ocean Hill-Brownsville struggle; what began as a possibility for effective community control ended with even more confusion and distrust of the public school system. Some of the "serious people" involved in this undertaking included the late Jim Williams (who served as the first editor of *Black News* from 1969–1972), the late Jim Dyson (whose art graced many covers of the newspaper), Antoinette Brown, Addie Rimmer, Maurice Fredericks, and Don Blackman.[5] Weusi argued that at the time *Black News* was created, there were too many "Negro" papers in circulation. The difference between a "Negro" paper and a "Black" paper was the issue of audience; Negro papers, according to Weusi, feared speaking directly to Black people because of what Whites might say and think, whereas a Black newspaper was going to interpret news and events from a Black perspective. In contrast to a "Negro paper," *Black News* would be guided by the seven principles of the Nguzo Saba (also known as the "seven principles of Blackness" which I discuss in the

Introduction) and reflecting a Black Nationalist ideology. This ideology has been defined as "the view that African Americans possess a distinct aesthetic sense of values, and communal ethos emerging from either, or both, their contemporary folkways and continental African heritage" (Brown, 2003, p. 6). At this point in time, the influence of Ron Karenga's US organization based in Los Angeles, California, had reached IBIs throughout the United States. Having an instrument that spoke to, for, and about Black perspectives was also a sign of the times. In context, *Black News* emerged after the assassinations of Malcolm X and Dr. Martin Luther King Jr. which left Black people throughout the United States demoralized and in some instances, adrift. Many African countries were claiming their independence after colonial rule and African, African American, and West Indian intellectuals were organizing pan-African organizations. In fact, the EAST became a member of the Congress of Afrikan Peoples (CAP) and the CAP newsletter, *Fundisha*, was included as an insert in *Black News* from July 1973 to April 1974.[6] Additionally, political tensions continued to escalate over the Vietnam War and the presidency of Richard Nixon (typically referred to in *Black News* as "Tricky Dick") memorialized in Muhammad Ali's famous quote, "No Vietnamese ever called me a nigger!" Many Black Americans also found themselves sympathetic to the Black struggle against South Africa's apartheid regime often seeing unsettling similarities between Black conditions in the United States and South Africa.[7] The founders of the newspaper wanted a safe space to engage in their concerns throughout the African Diaspora. *Black News* had few models for this style of reporting:

> For the first 45 minutes of the meeting, I introduced serious papers. There was this paper out of Boston, Massachusetts called *Rebellion News*. There was *The Black Panther Newspaper*. There was also *Muhammad Speaks* which was great for national issues but the local issues were aftermath.[8]
>
> (Jitu Weusi, interview, March 21, 2007)

The Black Panther, published weekly in Berkeley, California, was in its 11th volume by the time *Black News* came into existence. It frequently reprinted the Black Panther Party's "10 Point Program and Platform" in addition to platforms for Black Student Unions, the rules of the Black Panther Party as well as the "8 Points of Attention" and the "3 Main Rules of Discipline." *Muhammad Speaks,* "Dedicated to Freedom Justice and Equality for the so-called Negro," was published by the Nation of Islam in Illinois. More than a mouthpiece for the Nation of Islam, *Muhammad Speaks* reported stories that impacted Black people throughout the United States and abroad regardless of religious affiliation. The newspaper served as a model for many community publications. *Black News* employed the strategies of both newspapers by including both local and global issues concerning Black people and by using the method of listing demands and using cartoons or art to illustrate conditions and contradictions faced by Black people. Ultimately, *Black News* hoped to create a "tell it like it is" culture that would permeate the EAST organization:

> [*Black News*] was a hard hitting Black newspaper. A "tell it like it is" newspaper. We printed 5,000 of the first issue and it sold out in a week's time. We sold it in Brooklyn [and] at Liberation Books in Harlem. Students in the African American Student Association (ASA) were critical. We had about 70–100 students and they were responsible for distributing and selling the papers.
> (Jitu Weusi, interview, March 21, 2007)

A.S.A. was critical to the success of *Black News.* These passionate young people were supported by the African American Teachers Association.[9] Members of the A.S.A sold *Black News* in subway stations, at schools, and on the streets. Selling the paper was another way to get young people throughout New York City in dialogue with each other. Since the A.S.A. was an umbrella organization for Black high school students throughout Brooklyn, students had extensive networks that transcended neighborhoods and blocks. A.S.A students were learning that their voices and actions could create effective change. At the time of the formation of *Black News*, Black student organizations were springing up across the United States. The organization was full of passionate young people who were engaged in fighting for the inclusion of their voices and ideas in educational institutions. For example, the Black Panther newspaper included the "10 Point Program and Platform of the Black Student Unions" and supported a national headquarters for Black student organizations.[10] A similar struggle ensued across the ocean. Black student activists like the late Steve Biko were creating organizations like the South African Student Organization (SASO) and making their demands public in the midst of the apartheid regime. A.S.A. developed their platform and "The 15 Demands of the African American Students Association" was published within the first few months of the newspaper's existence (see Appendix B). At the top of this list of student demands was "No more automatic suspensions of [high school] students" quickly followed by "No more police or police aids inside NYC schools." Other demands demonstrated students' desire to give their parents a strong sense of entitlement at the school such as, "Open the schools daily to parent observation." Students also wanted the birthdays of Malcolm X, and Martin Luther King Jr. acknowledged and culturally relevant materials and school clubs. The final demand, written in all caps, showed students' sense of vulnerability in the school climate. Black youth simply wanted to attend schools where they were welcomed so they could receive their education:

15. THE REORGANIZATION OF THE HIGH SCHOOLS ALONG COMMUNITY LINES SO THAT BLACK STUDENTS WILL NOT BE FORCED TO GO TO SCHOOLS IN HOSTILE COMMUNITIES TO SEEK AN EDUCATION (FRANKLIN K. LANE, JOHN ADAMS, CARNARSIE, ETC.)

(African American Students Association, December 1, 1969, volume 1, no. 5, p. 6)

The *Black News* staff characterized these young people as "the new breed of Black youth" and felt a tremendous amount of responsibility for them ("The new breed of Black Youth," *Black News*, December 10, 1970, p. 2). To be sure, A.T.A held a series of evening classes for A.S.A students in order to supplement the public school curriculum. A.S.A staged their own strike in April 1969 which they called the "Spring Offensive" to protest the increasing presence of law enforcement in their schools as well as what students sensed as a lack of interest in their humanity by school administration and staff. The 15 demands, which were given to Mayor John Lindsay, were published by *Black News* and circulated widely in the community in line with the newspaper's mission. These actions would "build momentum" for a series of student protests. According to student reporters in *Black News*, the 15 demands "represented a minimum effort needed to correct injustices to black and other Third World students in the high schools" (p. 3). The December 10, 1970 issue of *Black News* dedicated the issue to "The Story of the African American Student Association and the students who build the organization."[11]

Written from the students' perspective, this issue documented their disappointment in public schools and teachers. Such frustration made their involvement with *Black News* and the EAST even more central to their lives.

Public school students were not the only active members of A.S.A. According to *Black News*, Black students at Our Lady of Victory (OLV), a Catholic school, were some of the most active sellers of the newspaper. In an article dedicated to OLV students, "Our Young Bloods at 'Our Lady of Victory,'" *Black News* acknowledged the dedication of the students as well as their teacher and urged other young people to develop papers:

> We also urge other Black students to check out the fine paper put out by the student body of [OLV], it's out of sight. Black students wherever they are must start creating their own means of communication in order to spread the Word and disseminate information on what's the Truth and what's lies. *Black News* and other publications can't do the job alone.
>
> ("Our young bloods at 'Our Lady of Victory,'"
> *Black News*, March 21, 1970, p. 5)

The education of Black youth and their families became a primary focus for *Black News* and the editorial staff used every issue to demonstrate this priority. Although OLV was a private Catholic school and *Black News* primarily focused on public schools, OLV student voices were on the pages signaling to readers that the need to bring young people together outweighed class distinctions.

"Mis-education," "Reeducation" and the Journey to Becoming "Correct"

At the beginning of its tenure *Black News* began its campaign to address what it referred to as the "mis-education" of Black and Puerto Rican youth in public schools by emphasizing the need to establish Independent Black Institutions (IBIs) and schools in particular. As early as the first issue, *Black News* set the stage for the Uhuru Sasa Academy—an Independent Black Educational Institution operating as a branch of the EAST organization. Using the A.S.A as its motivation, the vision was to have the revenue generated from the newspaper assist with the costs of operating the school. Moreover, *Black News* would serve as an instrument for promoting the school not only by emphasizing the 3-Rs in education —reading, writing and arithmetic—but also the implementation of the aforementioned fourth "R" for reciprocity. Black men, women, and children were challenged to name and define their purpose for learning and building literate lives as well as their commitment to strengthening their communities. Two articles in the sixth issue of *Black News* provided the rationale for these institutions using the metaphor of "a tiny blade of grass" emerging from an unexpected source in order "to feel the sun" (Tobias, 1969, p. 3). This "small seed," the Uhuru Academy, started as a Saturday School that met from 10am–5pm. Like many other Independent Black Educational Institutions, the Uhuru Academy began by offering Saturday classes in order to identify the needs of the community and establish a dedicated staff for a full-time school. This Saturday School, which held classes at 1231 Bedford Avenue, would eventually house programs for age groups 3–5, 6–8, 9–13, and later a secondary education program.

Uhuru Sasa was a strategic name for the school; to be sure, "Huru," is a Kiswahili word for "a free man, a person who is not a slave, free born or emancipated." However, "Uhuru," is defined as "freedom from slavery, liberty, emancipation" demonstrating movement from captivity to freedom. The founders of the school chose this name because they believed they were helping youth unearth their talents from the rubble of an oppressive public school structure that functioned as a "barrier" to their freedom: "The New York City Board of Miseducation, the New York City public school system is such a barrier. It shackles our children's minds, it destroys our children's minds" (Tobias, *Black News*, 1969, p. 3).

The term, "mis-education," borrowed from Carter G. Woodson's (1933) classic text *The Mis-education of the Negro*, was favored by Black Nationalists. It appeared throughout *Black News* and supporting materials from its sister institutions. Many of the *Black News* contributors employed the term "mis-education" to replace "education" in anything that involved the New York City public school system. Like Brooks's post-1967 discourse in the previous chapter, *Black News* writers frequently delineated between "Negroes" and "Blacks" arguing that Blacks were moving towards a self-awareness that many Negroes believed they did not need or want. Woodson argued that the Negro had been saturated by a discourse of inferiority that often led to a particular kind of paralysis:

> The thought of the inferiority of the Negro is drilled into him in almost every class he enters and in almost every book he studies. If he happens to leave school after he masters the fundamentals, before he finishes high school or reaches college, he will naturally escape some of this bias and may recover in time to be of service to his people.
>
> (Woodson, 1933/1969, p. 2)

Like Woodson, *Black News* believed that, as a result of racist policies and practices in public schools, Black youth were conditioned to surrender to the mythology of inferiority. Hence, *Black News* confronted and challenged this perception that this was an approach which was consistent with the historic role of the Black press, i.e, to "counter assumptions of African inferiority with displays of Black genius" (McHenry, 2002, p. 85). For example, *Black News* published an article entitled "Why your child gets low grades" discussing the policies and practices of the school guidance counselors who reportedly knew that a "grade ceiling" existed at some high schools with mostly Black and Puerto Rican students. "Mis-Guidance counselors," according to *Black News*, along with teachers and administrators were responsible for perpetuating the myth of Black inferiority: "This also reinforces the myth of Black intellectual inferiority since the educational institutions are still so grade conscious. We have got to put an end to this kind of educational oppression" ("Why your child gets low grades," April 10, 1970, volume 1, number 12, p. 3).

Uhuru Sasa, according to *Black News*, wanted to create a program to nurture and develop young black minds in the hope that students would become educators and reach out to the next generation. *Black News* further explained the need for the movement towards Independent Black Educational Institutions:

> The parents and teachers who started this school believe that the public school system can no longer serve our children adequately. We felt that a small seed could be planted. The first young bud would attempt to supplement the deficiencies of our youngsters and then this plant would eventually blossom out to become a Black school system. Our school system.
>
> (Tobias, 1969, p. 3)

Black News believed that the next logical step after the Ocean Hill-Brownsville struggle was to create a school and eventually an educational system independent of the public school system. In the same issue, Jitu Weusi used a narrative about his experiences as a junior high school history teacher at JHS 271. Weusi's account of his "big leap" to leave the New York City Board of "Mis-education" told the story of his suspension for playing Malcolm X's "The Ballot or the Bullet" speech over the school loudspeaker system (Campbell, December 19, 1969, p. 4). Although not documented in this particular article, Weusi also noted his efforts to organize a field trip to take students to a memorial in honor of Malcolm X had been branded subversive.[12] When Weusi could not get permission from the school administration to take students, he went directly to parents. Disregarding the administration's position, they gave him their permission. Weusi's "punishment" was being "demoted" to teaching elementary school even though his teaching license was specifically for "junior and senior high school social studies only." Weusi believed he was being used to control students at the elementary school who the administration and staff feared. Admittedly, Weusi "stuck pretty close to the script" during his first year of teaching in New York City schools in 1962. However, by February 1963, he saw that the curriculum was not working "It was a white curriculum and the kids were bored," Weusi explained and he knew he had to do something else for his students. Weusi explained the day he came across a poem entitled "What shall I tell my children who are Black?" by Margaret Burroughs, a close colleague of Gwendolyn Brooks, and how he was overwhelmed with its relevance to Black lives in the 1960s. Weusi decided to take Burroughs' poem and divide it into stanzas so that students could analyze the poem and create presentations in small groups. Weusi shook his head in disbelief as if he was reliving the moment: "These kids just took it and ran. It made all the difference" (Weusi, personal communication).

This situation further fueled his desire to see Brooklyn operate its own school. This "search for a new world" would lead to the creation of Uhuru Sasa School in Brooklyn's Bedford-Stuyvesant community (at that time Districts 13 and 16 of the school system). "Sasa," a Kiswahli adverb meaning "now, at this time, at present, in these days," was added to the existing name, "Uhuru." Uhuru Sasa emphasized the need for "Freedom Now," a slogan of impatience that was the essence of the Black Power Movement, in addressing the inadequate education of Black youth and the reeducation of their families and teachers in the existing system.

Uhuru Sasa officially opened as a full-time school in February 1970 and *Black News* dedicated numerous issues to recruiting students and teachers initially through its readership. The curriculum book, *Outline for a New African Educational Institution: The Uhuru Sasa School Program*, was printed by *Black News* (Figure 3.2) and the EAST

Figure 3.2 "Outline for a New African Educational Institution: The Uhuru Sasa Program" (1970).

for its "Black Nation Education Series" and included an open letter to parents:

> If students and their parents want Black teachers who are *educators* [original emphasis], then students, parents, and teachers alike must quit this white-racist system and begin to develop their own system. As have all ethnic and religious groups in this city. They have established and supported facilities that offer refuge, upholding and maintaining their values in this valueless society.
>
> (December 19, 1969, p. 4)

The vision for the Uhuru Sasa School was consistent with the values espoused by *Black News* which was to have a student-centered curriculum that inculcated Black youth with the value of self-reliance. This vision was also indicative of Black cultural nationalist ideologies which embraced the concept of self-determination.[13] This strategy, according to Campbell, was a "proper education" later used interchangeably with a "correct education" or "correct Black education" in the newspaper: "The curriculum, being arranged by the students, is geared to today's world . . . No games, but serious application to the question of proper education for Black youth" (p. 4).

Much of the *Black News* discourse surrounding Uhuru Sasa was derived from the teachings of Julius Nyerere, scholar and president of Tanzania, East Africa. Nyerere was instrumental in helping Tanzania, then Tanganyika, achieve independence from colonial rule and adamant about developing an effective education system defined by Tanzanians.[14] Weusi explained: "After Woodson, you didn't have directions. You didn't know where to go. Nyerere helped us understand where to go" (April 24, 2007). It was Nyerere's teachings of African independence and socialism that guided Weusi, the *Black News* editorial staff, and many workers in the EAST in creating a blueprint to combat mis-education and begin the reeducation process. Nyerere argued that one need not read Karl Marx to understand socialism but look to the traditional African society as a guide:

> The fact that pre-colonial Africa did not have "schools". . . . did not mean that the children were not educated. They learned by living and doing . . . Education was thus "informal": every adult

was a teacher to a greater or lesser degree. But this lack of formality did not mean that there was no education . . . Indeed, it may have made the education more directly relevant to the society in which the child was growing up.

(Nyerere, 1968, p. 45)

Nyerere emphasized in his essay entitled, "Education for Self-Reliance," that education must always have a purpose in the lives of people of African descent. In the fight to gain access to education, Nyerere argued that people of African descent had not taken time to properly shape and define "education" in the context of their lives. Weusi explained that *Black News*, the EAST, and the Uhuru Sasa School were initially a "reaction" to Ocean Hill-Brownsville. But over time these entities clarified and expanded their purpose and program. Using Woodson's and Nyerere's teachings as critical guides, *Black News* sought to redefine education in such a way that it would be relevant in the lives of its readership. One of the recurring themes in the newspaper was the notion that Black youth must receive a "proper" or "correct" education. John V. Churchville's lecture—originally published in *Black News* in 1970—underscored the relationship between a "Correct Black Education" and "Truth:" To this end, *Black News* published a transcript of a lecture given by John V. Churchville at Long Island University (L.I.U) entitled "On Correct Black Education." Churchville attempts to build a case for the need for such a process. Based in Philadelphia, where he was a founder of the Freedom Library Day School, Churchville also embraced the vision for a new world: "Correct Black Education sets up a system here that struggles against the opposing system by producing a new world" (Churchville, 1970, p. 3):

Correct Black Education says there needs to be a strict adherence to Truth alone. And the nationalism that we have says, "Yes, I'm Black, but I must adhere to the Truth first, because if I am going to be any good to Black people as a whole, I have got to be right!"

(Churchville, *Black News*, January 25, 1970, volume 1, number 8, p. 3)

Weusi and his colleagues did not feel that solely providing a "Correct Black Education" to the youth would suffice—especially if the values transmitted at Uhuru Sasa Shule were not cultivated in the home environment. Family involvement was key. In his column "Around Our Way," which I discuss later in this chapter, Weusi noted, "We have got to work on all parents, especially those over 30 years old. I hope all the youth that read *Black News* begin to educate their brainwashed parents" (*Black News*, July 6, 1970, volume 1, number 17, p. 4). Weusi explained that *Black News*, like Uhuru Sasa and all of the branches of the EAST, was part of a "family institution." Weusi continued: "By this, we mean that in order for our own program to be effective, the entire family must consent to reeducation" (Black Nation Education Series, 1970, p. 1). To be sure, *Black News* promoted adult programs heavily in its first year. One of the earliest adult learning opportunities, "The Black Study Circle," was advertised in the first issue of *Black News*. The purpose of the study circle was to hold small "discussion groups" to address "the Black Experiences, Afro-Black History, Black Literature, Blacks and Revolution and other related topics" ("Black Study Circle," *Black News*, October 1969, volume 1, number 1, p. 3). *Black News* described the general framework for these discussion groups including the importance of not having "teachers, instructors or lecturers" involved in order to avoid one person dominating the discussion. The circles were to have 7–8 people who would choose their reading material and share the labor of making "round robin" comments:

> Under no circumstances should the study group permit one man lecturing. If the group has not read, studied or understood the assigned topic, then round robin oral reading should take place at that meeting . . . No one should be excused from oral reading because of poor reading habits. The group's responsibility is to help the member improve in reading ability as well as in understanding the subject.
>
> (p. 3)

The Black Study Circle was a strong example of the values of learning that *Black News* and Uhuru Sasa believed to be part of a "correct" education for Black people. Such education included: (1) the creation of small learning communities; (2) a democratic sharing of the responsibility to name/define curriculum; (3) discouraging competition through a division of labor in the learning community; and (4) a communal sharing of responsibility in helping struggling readers and learners. In other words, group members were encouraged to move together rather than compete against each other. Once again, this format evolved from Nyerere's teachings which argued that education "must emphasize co-operative endeavor, not individual advancement" and avoid "intellectual arrogance" where one group (typically the "educated") learns to despise "those whose abilities are non-academic" leading to paralysis in nation-building:

> [Our educational system] has to foster the social goals of living together, and working together, for the common good. It has to prepare our young people to play a dynamic and constructive part in the development of a society in which all members share fairly in the good or bad fortune of the group, and in which progress is measured in terms of human well-being ... Our education must therefore inculcate a sense of commitment to the total community, and help the pupils to accept the values appropriate to our kind of future, not those appropriate to our colonial past.
>
> (Nyerere, 1968, p. 52)

In addition to The Black Study Circle, *Black News* did extensive advertising for the "African American Teachers Association Evening School of Knowledge." The idea behind the evening school was to give parents and educators opportunities to engage in some of the curriculum students would be exposed to at Uhuru Sasa. *Black News* printed elaborate calendars that often needed a full page; these calendars featured a range of offerings including: "practical" classes for adults seeking their G.E.D. High School Equivalency, "Practical journalism," and "Realistic Teacher Training." Classes, conducted by Black teachers in the A.T.A., were held Monday through Friday after work hours including sessions from 4–6, 5–7, 6–8, and 7–9 in the evening to meet the needs of working-class parents and full-time public school teachers.

Black News was relentless in its campaign to reeducate parents and adults. It not only held educational classes but used shaming techniques such as cautionary tales, as well as scathing critiques of parents who were not fully committed to their child's education. In the November issues leading up to the winter holiday season, *Black News* had a message for the "Christmas Nigger" for spending money he/she did not have on Christmas gifts:

Now you know that you only make 80 bucks for a whole long week. You were supposed to go up to school to find out why your kid can't read and you didn't ... But why waste time talking to you ... go downtown and throw away money you ain't got anyway. After all, God will take care of ... your child's inability to read and write.

("Christmas Nigger," *Black News,*
November 1969, p. 1)

Black News used many tactics to emphasize their commitment to educational issues. The public school system was not the only target for their education campaign. *Black News* ultimately held Black people solely responsible for the education of Black youth. In their article entitled, "The Games Black Folks Play," the editorial staff described the "ostrich" game as part of a shaming tactic:

Yes, Black Parent, you are Past Masters at the Game of Ostrich. You have, through ignorance, laziness, base fear and cowardice, given a white Board of Education, white U.F.T. teachers, white principals, and white policemen your full permission to destroy the minds and bodies of Black youth.

(Gilbert, *Black News,* January 10, 1970,
volume 1, number 7, p. 4)

Using the ostrich as a metaphor, *Black News* pointed fingers at Black parents and sought to shame them if they were not being proactive in their children's education and personal well-being. Like the newspaper's mission to "agitate, educate, and organize," *Black News* sought to upset parents enough to take action even if it meant being confrontational. Literacy and learning were the highest priorities for Black and Brown youth and *Black News* did not want anything or anyone contributing to the further mis-education of Black children. Survival of the community depended on literacy and learning. In an editorial entitled "Black Children ... The World is Yours," the editorial staff openly encouraged Black youth to make responsible decisions for themselves even if it meant going against parents and adults who were "not a part of that struggle" (*Black News,* February 15, 1970, volume 1, number 9, p. 8). Parents were also asked to be more critical and to resist accepting the public school's word about their children. *Black News* sought to foster a sense of entitlement among the readership. For example, in a plea to mothers in particular, the *Black News* staff encouraged parents of school-aged children to fully understand the context in which their child had been "suspended, excluded, or otherwise in trouble in school" before accepting that fate ("Understanding," *Black News*, November 15, 1969, volume 1, number 4, p. 3).

Black News also encouraged its readership to become educators and continuously used its pages to promote the need for independent Black schools. In a column entitled, "From Sisters to Sisters," Jul' Gilbert encouraged Black women to participate in a seminar series addressing parent involvement. Gilbert also invited female readers to join NAT's Women (as in Nat Turner) to learn about the importance of "community control": "We must construct and maintain our own educational facilities . . . We must establish a haven for the strong Black teachers— dynamic Black [teachers] who are being rendered useless by the system" (Gilbert, *Black News*, November 15, 1969, volume 1, number 4, p. 8).

Gilbert wrote other articles that attempted to influence Black women and mothers in particular. In her article entitled "The Soap Opera Syndrome," Gilbert addressed readers who found themselves addicted to daytime drama, "Look in the mirror, sister, you are not the white heroine of a television fantasy. You are a Black woman who should be fighting for survival in a racist, oppressive, decadent system" (Gilbert, *Black News*, November 15, 1969, volume 1, number 4, p. 3). In many ways, Gilbert's article reinforced the EAST organization's ideology that Blacks could only depend on themselves to cultivate their youth. Through the discourse of mis-education and reeducation, the newspaper upheld a "no excuse" policy. The newspaper's editorial staff did not want parents to bury their heads in the sand by playing the "Game of Ostrich," or get distracted by someone else's daytime drama on television.

Students from A.S.A. joined the *Black News* editorial staff in its efforts to reeducate parents. In "Understanding," the youth created a poem-like editorial which repeated the question, "MOTHERS, DO YOU REALLY UNDERSTAND?" challenging parents to probe into conflict between schools and their children ("Understanding," *Black News*, November 15, 1969, volume 1, number 4, p. 3). Parent organizations like the Parents Association of P.S. 305 also joined the reeducation campaign by publishing their concerns in *Black News*. The Parents Association argued that parents must "know" their rights and be "aggressive" about the educational process for their children:

We must stop leaving education in the hands of the so-called professionals. Some of them neither care nor do the really know how to teach . . . Our children need the kind of dedication that lasts beyond 3 o'clock and begins before 8:40. They need people who really care if they learn to read and count. They need patience and understanding, the kind of feeling you exhibit toward your own child.

(Parents Association of P.S. 305,
Black News, March 21, 1970, p. 4)

The Parents Association also published their list of demands of urban public schools, teachers, and staff:

1. [The teaching of the] True history of the Black Man
2. Teacher accountability for reading and math progress
3. End to suspensions
4. End to criminal acts against our children (rape, beatings)
5. Accountable Guidance Program in our schools (Elementary, Junior High School, and Senior High School).

Black News adopted the belief that anyone who came into contact with youth was an educator in his or her own way. Teaching and learning occurred around the clock and could not be neatly packed into a traditional school day. This value was not specific to *Black News* but to all of the entities of the EAST. This meant that everything published in *Black News*, even the advertisements, had to be consistent with this value system.

Preserving "Black Dignity": Advertising in *Black News*

Advertisements in *Black News* were a part of building a particular kind of cultural literacy among its readership. These advertisements had to adhere to the newspaper's commitment to reeducate youth and adults including goods and services that followed the seven principles or the Nguzo Saba. Therefore these ads tell part of the story of the newspaper and its commitment to the preservation of "Black Dignity": "We're choosey about ads. If they don't satisfy Black Dignity, they don't satisfy *Black News*" ("Black News of Bedford Stuyvesant," October 1969, volume 1, number 1, p. 1). *Black News* referenced contradictions in Negro publications that featured positive articles about Black people but who also relied on hair straightening products, skin brightening creams, alcohol and tobacco products to sustain their newspaper circulation:

> Throughout the life of *Black News*, the foregoing features of the publication, coupled with local and consistent advertisers were responsible for its endurance and readership. Parenthetically, it is important to note that advertisers too were conscientiously held to a cultural and value-based standard.
>
> (Konadu, 2005, p. 42)

Advertisements were introduced methodically in the paper first appearing as lists including the addresses, phone numbers and store hours for restaurants, barber shops, hair styling salons, flowers, gifts, fashions, electronics and record shops. The first large-scale advertisement, Phillips Barber Shop, appeared in the fourth issue of *Black News* on the back cover. Phillips Barber Shop in Brooklyn declared its commitments to natural styles:

> Want to have that real black and beautiful look? Then you want to see Sister Phillips at the Phillips Barbershop.

Cary's Exclusive Barbershop on Nostrand Avenue in Brooklyn followed Phillips Barbershop's lead by boasting, "Specializing in everything to accent your natural beauty" (*Black News*, April 10, 1970, p. 2). In subsequent ads, Phillips Barbershop added "Permanents and Relaxers Removed" solidifying their commitment to Black people's natural hair and rejection of hair straightening chemicals (*Black News*, May 29, 1970, p. 15). In addition to barbershops, variety stores and gift shops largely supported *Black News*. Woody's R&B Variety Afro-Shop advertisements, which often included a photograph of people on the bus with the caption "Going to see Bro. Woody," boasting to have "Everything in Red, Black, and Green" known as nationalist colors. Woody's seemed particularly proud to carry a surplus of "Liberation Flags" as well as incense at affordable prices. Nyabinghi's African Gift Shop first appeared in a full-page back cover advertisement in *Black News*. The ad, which depicted an outline of the continent of Africa with a list of items they sold including drums, carvings, garments, greeting cards, and fabric to name a few, proudly announced "Culture has arrived in Brooklyn" (September 5,

1970). By 1973, readers saw an increase in advertisements for food co-operatives, natural food stores, and healthy eating in general. The EAST had its own food cooperative called Kununuana Co-Op located on 1115 Fulton Street in Brooklyn. In the advertisement, the co-op's name was written inside an Egyptian Ankh symbol representing eternal life with the phrases "Food for Life" and "Shopping in Tradition" written along side of it. Some of the items listed included organic eggs, brown rice and sugar, and fresh fruits and vegetables. *Black News* wanted its readership to know where to go for any services they needed and also to urge readers to support Black-owned and operated businesses that recognized "Black" consciousness.

Black-owned and Black-operated bookstores were also frequent supporters of *Black News*. Many of these stores carried *Black News* as well as *The Black Panther* and *Muhammad Speaks* newspapers. In particular, Liberation Bookstore in Harlem, New York was the first bookstore to advertise in *Black News* with a space a little larger than a standard business card advertisement. Liberation Bookstore's logo showed an arm reaching up with a shackle around the wrist. The chain, which was broken, had "If you don't know, learn. If you know, teach" written along the links of the chain. The copy read:

> Have you ever read the "Autobiography of Malcolm X" for the second time? Or have you picked up on "Wretched of the Earth" by Fanon? Or poems by Don L. Lee? If not you'll find all these books and more at one of the great Black bookstores in the country . . . the Liberation Bookstore.
>
> (*Black News*, November 15, 1969, volume 1, number 4)

Additionally, bookstore advertisements served as reminders to *Black News* readers about who and what they should be reading. According to Liberation Books, *The Autobiography of Malcolm X* was considered required reading for Blacks; however, it was not only to be read once but multiple times. Fanon's (1963) *Wretched of the Earth* was purposely situated next to *The Autobiography of Malcolm X*. Born in Martinique, Fanon was known for his scathing critiques of colonialism and the effect it had on people of African descent. In fact, *Black News* often integrated Malcolm X and Fanon quotes throughout the newspaper. Although located in Harlem at the corner of Lenox Avenue (now Malcolm X Boulevard) and 131st Street, the bookstore was successful in forging relationships between Blacks in the different boroughs. It seemed appropriate that Liberation Bookstore's advertisement appeared on the same page as a featured poem by Don L. Lee who was not only known as a poet and writer but a co-founder of the Institute for Positive Education (IPE) in Chicago, Illinois (discussed in Chapter 2) which housed the New Concept Development Center, Third World Press and the editor of *Black Books Bulletin*. Lee's voice was consistently present throughout the tenure of *Black News*.

Black News returned the support of its advertisers by reviewing events. For example, when Kimako's Tea Room and bookstore hosted a "book party" for Amiri Baraka, formerly LeRoi Jones, *Black News* featured a review of the event:

> The IMAMU AMIRI BARAKA jumped into his TERRIBLE-NESS. With his SUPERBAD poetry. The first poem dealt with "the me(s)." LEROI has gotten into a very deep sound-thing with his poetry. He is writing the sounds of black folks. The jazz. The blues. The rhythms. His verses ring with music. Our music. And our thoughts. BARAKA is a genius. A genius of black music. Of black sounds. And a teacher . . . Oh yes, the book party was most successful.
>
> (Sis. Ruby Saunders, *Black News*, March 28, 1971, p. 22)

The Freedom Bookstore, located in Brooklyn, was another bookstore that featured author events. Freedom Bookstore's advertisements announced their forthcoming autograph party and poetry reading series featuring poets such as Sonia Sanchez reading from her book *Liberation Poems*, and *Homecoming* (1969) published by Dudley Randall's Broadside Press, and Nikki Giovanni reading from *Black Feeling, Black Talk, Black Judgment* (1970). There were also "autograph parties" for authors of cookbooks focusing on African-centered cuisine including *Vibration Cooking, Or the Travel Notes of a Geechee Girl* (1970) by Vertamae Smart-Grosvenor and the *African Heritage Cookbook* (1971) by Helen Mendes. The mutual respect between *Black News* and local bookstores was also evident in other sections of the newspaper. Although the National Memorial Bookstore in Harlem did not officially advertise in *Black News*, Weusi informed readers about the bookstore's historic role:

Why and Who ... is trying to put Bro. Lewis Michaux of National Memorial Bookstore (125th and 7th) out of business? Bro. Michaux and his enterprise have been responsible for opening the eyes of many of our leaders (past, present, and future). Your writer brought his 1st Black books in Mr. Michaux's shop some 9 years ago and this brilliant old brother has never stopped selling and distributing books by and about African people. SUPPORT YOUR BLACK BOOKSTORES!

(Weusi, *Black News*, January 28, 1974, p. 12)

The all-important continuum of Black art from literature to theatre and music was defined through *Black News'* advertisements as well. The newspaper advertised extensively for theatre companies throughout New York City who produced and performed works by Black playwrights and/or about Black people. One of the first theatre advertisements appeared in the seventh issue of *Black News*. It featured the work of Amiri Baraka. The Third World Cultural Organization, who referred to Baraka as a "Famous Author, Poet, Playwright, Blackman," announced it would be showing "Four One-Act Black Plays" by his performance group called the Spirit House Movers and Players. Yusef Iman, a consistent performer at the EAST along with the Weusi Kuumba, and the Young Spirit were on this bill as well. In this same issue, the African American Teachers Association announced its fundraiser for the Uhuru Sasa School featuring "A Season in the Congo" written by Aime Césaire."[15] Born in Martinique, Césaire was not only known as a poet, playwright but also for his activism in the "Negritude" movement which sought to promote Black pride and dignity initially among the Francophone Caribbean and Africa. "A Season in the Congo" focused on the life of Congolese leader Patrice Lumumba who led the struggle against Belgium's imperialism in the Congo. Performed by The Harlem School of the Arts, a second production of "A Season in the Congo" also served as a fundraiser for Uhuru Sasa Shule.[16] Many other playhouses advertised in *Black News*, including The New Lafayette Theatre in Harlem, New York who encouraged readers to schedule visits to "chat with company members" (*Black News*, July 23, 1970, p. 14), the aforementioned Kimako's Black Theatre and Health Foods (which was also known as the Egyptian Tea Room) also sold dashikis, books, records, incense and jewelry and Oomboola's Playhouse in Brooklyn who featured dance, arts, dashikis and books (*Black News*, September 5, 1979, pp. 12–13).

Although theatrical productions were advertised frequently in the early issues of *Black News*, it was not until one year into the newspaper's existence that the editorial staff explicitly addressed issues concerning the role of "Black Theatre," noting that theatre companies were competing against each other to bear this title: "The irony of this situation is that the sought after title 'The Black Theatre' can only be given, or rather bestowed by the black community, which doesn't intend to give that title to one little group" ("Black Theatre," *Black News*, September 26, 1970, volume 1, number 21, p. 15).

"Black Theatre," or plays written by, for, and about people of the African Diaspora, was a large part of the cultural literacy *Black News* wanted its readers to have. However, in this editorial, the staff made it clear that the "community doesn't want a Black Theatre but rather an all-embracing concept of Black Art." For this reason, and the sake of unity *Black News* objected to promoting one playhouse over another hereby applying the teachings of Nyerere.

The ideology around "Black Art" was also embedded in the EAST's programming. Originally known as "Black Experience in Sound," the EAST primarily featured prominent Jazz musicians who donated their performances as fundraisers for Uhuru Sasa Shule:

> During the *Black Experience in Sound*, the musicians, who were also extremely politically conscious, were called "messengers" due to their "teachings" between musical sets. To some, these musicians were the "musical proof that the politics of Black Nationalism and Nationhood [were] being practiced in all walks of life."
>
> (Konadu, 2005, p. 3)

Most of the back covers of *Black News* served as ad space for these concerts that were held at the EAST on 10 Claver Place (Figure 3.3). The first of many back cover announcements, *Black News* urged readers to "support the educational and cultural works of Black people" every Friday and Saturday evening with two shows nightly (*Black News*, January 25, 1970). The announcement noted that "10 Claver Place" was the "home" to the ASA, *Black News*, Uhuru Sasa, and noted "home-cooked meals and non-alcoholic beverages" would be served. Some of the featured artists or messengers included Gary Bartz Ntu Quintet (Bartz later recorded a song called "Uhuru Sasa"), Billy Harper Sextet,

Figure 3.3 Sample back cover of *Black News*.

Eddie Gale's "Ghetto Music" and "Black Rhythm Happening," Joe Lee Wilson, Carlos Garnett and the Universal Black Force, Elvin Jones, Sun Ra and his "Space Arkestra," Yusef Lateef, Betty Carter, McCoy Tyner, Lee Morgan, Freddie Hubbard, Leon Thomas, Pharoah Sanders, Doug and Jean Carn, Joe Bataan, and Max Roach. Poets and artists such as Amiri

Baraka, Sonia Sanchez, the Last Poets, and Yusef Iman and Weusi Kuumba sometimes joined jazz musicians on stage as did Uhuru Sasa students to read their poetry. Musicians and poets were essentially donating their time to raise money for the EAST accepting little to no compensation. This act of reciprocity was also evident in the "Around Our Way" column that became the core of the newspaper and synthesized the events at the various EAST entities for the *Black News* readership.

Building Community "Around Our Way"

The regular column "Around our way" became the heart of *Black News*; it presented the practical applications of the newspaper's mission to "agitate, educate and organize." Here Weusi synthesized all of the ideas embraced by *Black News* and the other entities of the EAST. As the headmaster of Uhuru Sasa Shule, Weusi also used "Around our way" to communicate the "happenings" at the school. In one of his first columns, which appeared in the January 10, 1970 issue of *Black News*, Weusi warned the readers in all caps, "WATCH OUT FOR THE NEW BLACK POLITICS UNFOLDING IN NYC" (p. 4). Weusi expected his readers to become informed and then engaged in the political issues that impacted public schools and used his column as a bulletin board of sorts to announce meetings, conferences and report on them afterwards. Most visible was the way Weusi used his column to support Independent Black Institutions. For example, he expressed his concern that the Decentralization Bill following the Ocean Hill-Brownsville struggle was a "scheme that holds nothing for our children." Weusi then used this point to promote Independent Black Institutions (IBIs): "Begin to build independent schools *NOW!* The public schools are like a sinking ship, too far gone to save with any measure of assistance" ("Black children . . . the world is yours," *Black News*, February 15, 1970, volume 1, number 9, p. 5).

Weusi encouraged readers to become an active part of the *Black News* family rather than passive readers. The tone of his column carried a persuasive tenor with assertive honesty expressing his disappointment in the lack of activism of readers. However, "Around our way" also conveyed a profound sense of love for Black youth and those who were willing to struggle on their behalf. In many ways, the "Around our way" column expressed the thought that true revolution was the creation of educated, literate, and self-sustaining Black families. Weusi openly and often expressed his disdain for "talkers" who mindlessly chanted "revolution":

> With revolutionary action you don't need to *say* [original emphasis] a damn thing. Just do what you're talking about without all the talking. The Black Revolution is about *doing* and not *talking* [original emphasis] . . . At *Black News* we want doers not talkers.
>
> (Campbell, *Black News*, March 21, 1970, p. 14)

Continuing the legacy of words inciting action, Weusi spoke to the need for an active readership. Weusi ended this particular column by restating the purpose of *Black News* and punctuating the column with: "TODAY— 6 MONTHS LATER, WE ARE STILL STANDING ON THE SAME PLATFORM" (p. 14).

Wesui was particularly astute at referencing books and other texts in his column demonstrating his own passion for reading while simultaneously modeling his belief in the power of literate practices. In an issue of *Black News* dedicated to Malcolm X entitled "He Lives," Weusi discussed his reading process of *The Autobiography of Malcolm X*:

> Each Feb. 21st after all the Rallies have been held and all the speeches made honoring the memory of El Hajj Malik Shabazz (Malcolm X), I usually retreat to the quiet solitude of my soul for a real memorial tribute. I begin to take stock of what I have contributed for the advancement of self and kind during the past year . . . then I read several chapters of the "Autobiography" and come away feeling meek and humble. At that point I rededicate myself and my every thought once again.
>
> (Big Black, *Black News*, February 25, 1971, p. 6)

Once again, Weusi made a distinction between talking and doing. It was, for many, fashionably Black to attend Malcolm X rallies and tributes. However, Weusi reminded readers that the tributes should lead to some kind of action. For Weusi, it meant revisiting *The Autobiography of Malcolm X* in order to recharge or "rededicate." One of the most compelling elements of "Around our way" was that readers could really hear Weusi's positive voice and personal struggle to remain hopeful that education, economics, and housing issues would get better. In the January 1972 issue of *Black News*, Weusi gave a subtitle to this particular column, "1972—The Year of Black Politics?" Before he began to write, Weusi included a passage from *David Walker's Appeal of 1830* (see Chapter 1) in which Walker had urged people of African descent to fight against enslavement and the dehumanization of African people. Weusi wanted readers to connect Walker's appeal ("Can our condition be any worse? Can it be more mean and abject?") with the economic, social, and political climate of the early 1970s:

> These words written by [David Walker] who mysteriously died in 1830 can serve as the battle cry for 1972, the year of Black politics. Every junkie should read these words and black intellectuals too. Most street bloods understand and are poised and ready.
>
> (Big Black, *Black News*, January 1972, p. 11)

Weusi utilized this passage to begin his analysis regarding the scarcity of Black owned businesses in the community, the drug crisis or "The Dope Age" that was plaguing Black and Latino communities, and the upcoming local and national elections. Arguing that it was "time to get down to business," Weusi asked readers to consider the words of Frederick Douglass in his essay "What is your Fourth of July to Me?" (p. 13) examining the hypocrisy of a celebration of independence in the life of an American Slave.[17]

Weusi not only used historical texts as examples of how words should incite action and eventually change in the conditions for Blacks but also employed quantitative data generated from reports and other publications in his column. In the February 1972 issue of *Black News*, Weusi recommended the readership examine a booklet entitled "The Fact Sheets on Institutional Racism" compiled by the Foundation for Change in New York City. According to Weusi, this publication documented "White control and Black oppression in the areas of economy, health, insurance, housing, education, media, government and census" (*Black News*, February, 1972, p. 27). In many ways, Weusi offered briefings about these publications citing specific social data; for example, he reported that more that 70% of New York State's prison population was non-white but that 98% of the correction officers were white according to the Foundation. In the March 15, 1973 issue of *Black News*, Weusi began "Around our way" with a nod to the Fleischman Report as well as an article that appeared in the *New York Times* focusing on the "urban school problems" existing in Philadelphia. This *New York Times* article, "Urban School Problems Intensify in Philadelphia" asserted that the crisis in Philadelphia public schools was merely a reflection of a larger crisis in other urban cities such as New York City, Chicago and Detroit (King, 1973). The article cited white flight to parochial schools and the deficit in the school budget as two of the main issues contributing to school failure. Once again, Weusi used these reports to urge readers to support independent Black schools:

> In Philadelphia, in New York and Detroit, Chicago and else-where we need revolutionary Black Freedom Schools. We've started here in Brooklyn with such fantastic Black Academies of positive education as UHURU SASA Shule, WEUSI SHULE and several others . . . We call these schools liberated zones of the African community since they are free from the intellectual contamination of white America. So the slogan has become "Remove your child from the war zone (public school) into the Liberated Zone." The future of our race will be decided by what you do about the education of our youth.
> (Weusi, *Black News*, March 15, 1973, p. 27)

No stranger to education and controversy, Weusi's parents were American Communists in the 1950s. Weusi's mother, Mardesta Stewart, was a "staunch community person" and advocate of education. Weusi's father, Robert Campbell, was into politics and "knew a lot of people." As a child, Weusi worked with some of his cousins at a newspaper stand in Brooklyn, New York, where he started to become an avid reader. Another major influence in Weusi's life was the author John Oliver Killens who was his neighbor in Brooklyn. Killens often took time to "play ball" with the young men on Weusi's block. One day, Weusi recalled Killens giving copies of his novel *Youngblood* to all of the young people in the neighborhood. Weusi and his peers were in awe that they actually knew a writer and admired the kindness Killens displayed. The sharing and exchanging of the written and spoken word followed Weusi into his career as an educator, and eventually as a community journalist for *Black News*. Weusi understood the Black Nationalist movement and thus *Black News* to be a literacy-centered movement:

The movement was a literacy-based movement. What do I mean by that? I mean that between *Muhammad Speaks*, the Panther Party newspaper, *Black News*. . . you had to read in order to keep up with what was going on. *You had to read to keep up with what was going on* [Weusi's repetition for emphasis]. Reading became a necessary tool in the struggle. It shaped every discussion we had, "Man, did you see so and so's column in *Muhammad Speaks*?" "Did you see what what's his name said in the Black Panther paper man?" "Did you read about such and such?"

(Jitu Weusi, interview, April 24, 2007)

Weusi's claim that the Black Nationalist movement was a literacy-based movement was evident throughout his tenure as the "Around our way" columnist. Literacy and knowledge were the key tenets of revolutionary action. One had to be well read in literature, and history but most importantly one had to be willing to organize and take action. In addition to preserving the legacy of the Ocean Hill-Brownsville struggle and supporting *Black News*'s campaign to address education issues, "Around our way" began the process of reeducation by promoting the value of reading, thinking critically and dialoguing with others.

"From There to Here": The Making of Revolutionary Literacies

Black News ceased publication around 1984. However, prior to that year the newspaper was not published as consistently as it had been from 1969–1974. According to Weusi, Uhuru Sasa Shule closed its doors in 1986 and the EAST closed soon after (Konadu, 2005). The African International Arts Festival, which began as a street festival on Claver Place in front of the EAST to raise money for Uhuru Sasa Shule, is still a thriving Brooklyn institution nearly 40 years later. Weusi explained that *Black News*, the EAST, and Uhuru Sasa may have been too progressive for the time period:

We were about 20 years ahead of our time but I think we had a lot of significance. *Black News*, Uhuru Sasa, and the EAST showed a few things. We proved that Blacks can still educate Blacks. We proved we still had something to offer the curriculum. The EAST was just 20 years ahead of its time and the Black middle class wasn't ready. People tell me all the time they

wish we had [*Black News*, Uhuru Sasa, and the EAST] now . . .
But at the same time we needed it to get from there to here. We
needed it to get from there to where we are standing now.

(Jitu Weusi, interview, April 24, 2007)

In a study of an all-Black school during the legalized segregation in
North Carolina, Siddle Walker (1996) posits that the teachers at the
Caswell County Training School demonstrated an ethic of care that
blurred boundaries between school and home. Teachers recreated
families through the use of homerooms and carried high expectations of
their students. Independent Black Educational Institutions employed
this same ideal—to nurture young people and their families. Weusi's
understanding of what *Black News*, the EAST, and Uhuru Sasa contributed to education embrace what is now referred to as culturally
relevant pedagogy (Irvine, 2002, 2003; Ladson-Billings, 2001, 2005) as
well as student-centered teaching and learning. In this chapter I
examined how the values of Black consciousness, literacy, education,
and self-reliance put forth by *Black News* were indicative of other
Independent Black Institutions. These institutions were organized by
poets, writers, and lovers of words and language like Weusi. The Institute
for Positive Education in Chicago, Illinois, housed the New Concept
Development Center, Third World Press and published *Black Books
Bulletin*. East Palo Alto, California, was home to the Nairobi Day Schools
and Nairobi College. Ahidiana, co-founded by Kalamu ya Salaam,
operated in New Orleans, Louisiana, and Amina and Amiri Baraka
chartered Newark's African Free School in Newark, New Jersey. And the
aforementioned Shule Jumamose in Sacramento, California, co-founded
by Cheryl Fisher, Bertha Gorman, Martha Reid, and LeRoi Willis. There
were many others and the Council of Independent Black Institutions
still serves as an umbrella organization to African-centered, and Black
community schools.[18] IBIs have created a blueprint for literacy-centered
events in out-of-school contexts in the 20th and 21st century. Many of
these intergenerational venues have their own unique qualities but also
draw on a legacy of literacy and activism.

CHAPTER 4

"The Song Is Unfinished"

Soldiering in Participatory Literacy Communities

Poet and activist Ruth Forman began to re-imagine herself and other young poets of the late twentieth century as "the young magicians." Unlike the typical image of magicians with "trick canes," Forman contends that "with a mere wave of the pen" these young magicians can "transform grey concrete to yellow brick roads." Emerging from a tradition of poet activism, Forman was a student in June Jordan's "Poetry for the People[1]" program at the University of California, Berkeley. An obvious nod to Marcus Garvey's newspaper section dedicated to poetry, "Poetry for the People" was a program in which undergraduates took a three-semester course learning how to craft their poetry and work with high school students and teachers in public schools throughout the San Francisco/Bay Area. Forman's proclamation "Look at me/I am we" in a poem tribute to the evolution of Black poets and writers conveys that she and her fellow young magicians understand their place in a long line of literate and literary practices and is best summarized in one line, "we are new buds upon the highest branches." Who are these "young magicians" that Forman writes so bravely about and what are their institutions for reading, writing, speaking, and "doing" the word? And most importantly, what are the literate and literary traditions from which these "new buds" emerge? Who are their mentors and advocates? The previous chapters in this book introduced the historical predecessors to the "young magicians" and the literate and literary traditions from which these "new buds" emerge. Poet activists like Gwendolyn Brooks, educators and community organizers like Jitu Weusi, and Independent Black Institutions such as *Black News*, and its umbrella organization the EAST demonstrate that the recent renaissance of spoken and written words driven by community action is not new. However, as Forman offered, there are indeed "new buds" on the "highest branches" of these historical institutions.

The purpose of this chapter, then, is to examine the cultural practices of Participatory Literacy Communities—PLCs—(Fisher, 2003a, 2003b, 2004, 2006a, 2006b, 2007b) or institutions created by Black people to provide a forum for Black readers, writers, and lovers of words and language. These are communities that are constantly evolving while being defined and redefined by participants to meet the needs of emerging writers and expressionists. Although the definition of PLCs has evolved since this research was first introduced, there are salient characteristics that undergird the nature of these spaces. PLCs include venues, activities, and events that encourage reading (local writers and poets as well as those recognized nationally and internationally), writing (poetry, prose, music), dialogue ("open mics," exchanges with featured authors), and community action (education, housing, local government, inequities in the justice system). Like IBIs, PLCs take place in settings that have multiple purposes; for example, the spoken word poetry venues in the original study took place in cafés and restaurants that hosted related programming including film nights featuring Black, West Indian and African filmmakers, study groups, and music of the African Diaspora. PLCs complicate fixed notions "performer/reader" and "audience" because there is an expectation that everyone present must contribute in some way; in sum, the audience is not allowed the luxury of being merely entertained or passive. This tradition, largely referred to as "call and response," is when "the speaker's solo voice alternates or is intermingled with the audience's response" (Smitherman, 1999, p. 64). Ultimately this tradition reinforces the communal values associated with literacy as well as the focus on dialogue and exchange. Drawing from ethnographic research I conducted in Black-owned and operated bookstores events and spoken word poetry "open mic" events, this chapter examines how the values of self-determination, reciprocity, and inter-and cross-generational dialogue continue to be at the core of literacy learning for people of African descent. I begin with Black bookstores and open mic events because these spaces continue to preserve the rich tradition of reciprocity found in the learning communities created by enslaved Africans in the Americas, literary societies during Reconstruction, the writing workshops organized by Gwendolyn Brooks, and the forum that *Black News* sought to create for Black youth, their parents and educators. Black-owned and operated bookstores have a legacy of providing Black writers and readers with books, recordings, cards, calendars, and art that were unavailable in other bookstores, and city, school, and university libraries. Most importantly, Black bookstores have hosted Black writers and poets while opening their doors to a variety of community forums beyond the commercial aspect of selling merchandise as evidenced by the bookstores advertised in *Black News*.

"We Want to Encourage Elders and Children to Come"

In a study that documented book vendors who operated on the sidewalks of New York's Greenwich Village, Duneier (2000) shares the stories of men and women who not only sold books and magazines at their tables, but also the forums that ensued as a result of the interaction at these spaces. Hakim, an African American vendor in Duneier's study who largely sold "Black books" or a "constellation of related subjects and issues" pertaining to people of African descent created a culture of discussion and debate at his book table (p. 24). Clients of all ages sought Hakim's consultation about what books they should read next and he especially cultivated a relationship around the readings with an emerging reader who worked nearby. Drawing on Anderson's (1992, 2000, 2003) research with inner-city neighborhoods, Duneier employs the term "old head" to describe Hakim's ability to share wisdom and insight with the novice readers who frequent his table. An "old head," according to Anderson, is an elder man or woman in the African American community who uses storytelling and wit to share and exchange information. The old head's style and creativity with language and stories often appealed to the younger people he or she hoped to reach. Once again the value of reciprocity—that is elders exchanging information with young people in hopes to encourage them—is evidenced by Anderson's work. However, Anderson argues that the introduction of drug culture and a pervasive generation gap between elders and youth in inner-city Black communities in many ways neutralized the power of the old heads. Participants in PLCs have begun to reestablish the role of the old heads;

in these spaces elders listen to emerging voices and make room for them at the table. The organizers and participants in these events embody the ideology of Brooks and the culture of *Black News* in that they feel the urgency in maintaining relevance with young people. This ideology permeated the Poetry on a Saturday Afternoon (POSA) event at Carol's Books in Sacramento, California. Organized by a mother and daughter poetry team, Straight Out Scribes (SOS), POSA's methods and practices were direct descendants of the literacy activism demonstrated in Brooks's work with young writers and *Black News*'s outreach to youth.

Carol's Books which housed POSA was not always a "Black bookstore." Carol McNeal, the founder and co-owner along with her husband and children, had a book stall in a Sacramento shopping area where she carried a variety of books from 1984–1989. When the McNeal family relocated from Ohio to California in the mid-1950s, Mrs. McNeal was a nurse and Mr. McNeal was a doctor. Reading was always Mrs. McNeal's "hobby" and she specifically recalled reading about George Washington Carver and always being interested in African American biographies as opposed to works of fiction. However, it was still not her intention to establish what became known as Sacramento's premier Black bookstore. Much like Gwendolyn Brooks, Mrs. McNeal had an encounter with emerging scholars that began to influence the way she saw her work. During the time she operated her book stall, Mrs. McNeal started attending free classes at the Oak Park Community Center, not far from where the Oak Park School for Afro American Thought and Shule Jumamose were located. These classes were taught by Brother Imhotep, a community scholar who established an African centered church, Wo'se Community Church, in Sacramento. According to Mrs. McNeal, Brother Imhotep's classes were held three times a week and much of the teachings focused on Egypt's contributions to the world:

> They were so enriching and [Brother Imhotep] could refer you to books that you could read for yourself and then I discovered that he had been a student of Dr. Oba T'Shaka at San Francisco State. Dr. T'Shaka would eventually come and sign books and give lectures here at the store and it just became a really enlightening period. So then the focus on African American, Native American and some Hispanic books just began to take place.
>
> (interview, January 23, 2002)

As Mrs. McNeal started reading more and interacting with this newer generation of scholars, the focus of Carol's Books changed. In 1989, when the store reopened in the Lanai Shopping Center as an independent bookstore, Carol's Books became one of the city's greatest resources for not only books by, for, and about African, African American, and Caribbean people but also for multicultural literature. Mrs. McNeal believed that Carol's Books "just happened":

> I've always felt the store wasn't really mine. It's not for me. I'm just an instrument for it to be here, and I know that here is a force other than my own that is guiding it . . . I would like for more people to know that it's here so they could learn and discover the richness of their heritage . . . I have learned to accept the fact that those who need to know are here and those who don't aren't ready.

Mrs. McNeal also believed that meeting Staajabu and V.S. Chochezi, the mother and daughter poetry team also known as Straight Out Scribes, was a divine meeting. Mrs. McNeal admired Staajabu's activism around organizing literary events around Sacramento and invited SOS to establish a program at Carol's Books. POSA first began under the name of "African Expressions Poetry Sessions" in 1990–1991. Prior to hosting events at public venues, Staajabu held gatherings for writers and poets in her home. A former member of Ron Karenga's US organization and an early pioneer of organizing for the freedom of Mumia Abu Jamal, Staajabu always saw writing as being inextricably linked to activism. "I was writing to defend myself," explained Staajabu when asked about her writing career which was further inspired by reading the newspaper, getting an "attitude," and writing a letter to the editor nearly every day for two years.

Similar to Hakim's book table, Staajabu and V.S. Chochezi considered POSA to be a "Black reading" where people of African descent could talk about their experiences in a comfortable and supportive setting. Staajabu further contended that a Black reading was a place where she could advocate literacy learning for young people and the importance of exposure to words and language through featured writers and poets:

> We want to encourage elders and children to come, especially children, because we think they benefit so much from the poetry,

and we want them to experience what you can do with words and how delightful it is to be around people who love the spoken word and the written word, because they'll be in a bookstore, and the reason why we keep doing it is so people will come to Carol's.

(interview, January 10, 2002)

Staajabu's journalist background shaped POSA; the entire event served as a living text; it was a place to gather information, share editorials and functioned like a living and breathing local newspapers. At POSA, elders provided youth with an opportunity to experience not only the words themselves, but to see people and images who were readers, writers, speakers, and singers while sitting among the literature and being allowed to handle the books that were for sale in the store. Staajabu exemplified this through her relationship with her daughter and POSA co-host, V.S. Chochezi. At POSA, young people were exposed to language and print through the public readings and also by being surrounded by books. Many families brought their children to POSA with the strong belief that their children would learn to be skilled readers and writers by watching adults engage in discussions around poetry and literature (Fisher, 2003a, 2006a, 2007b). However, exposure was only the first level.

Straight Out Scribes formatted POSA strategically so that the audience participants were involved rather than sitting passively. POSA activities culminated in an invitation for audience participants to share the stage of the featured writer. First, the featured author would have between 45–50 minutes to share his or her work. Authors varied in their delivery and style, and often asked for audience participation. Second, there was time for community announcements in which everyone was invited to share upcoming events or introduce issues or concerns. Straight Out Scribes began a game to get the audience involved called "Know your Peeps," using a deck of cards with noted photographs of African, African American and West Indian writers, historians, leaders, and scholars. Staajabu or V.S. Chochezi would show the picture and the audience participants were expected to call out the name of the person. After the community announcements, there would be a "Mumia Abu-Jamal update," in which Staajabu would share any new information about Native American, Latino, and African American political prisoners throughout the United States in addition to letters from Abu-Jamal.

Participants were encouraged to read the community newspaper, *Because People Matter*, and would circulate copies to everyone. Here, Straight Out Scribes encouraged participants to write letters and poetry, and to use their "voices" to articulate their concerns. The last part of POSA was an "open mic," time for writers or poets to share their work with the Carol's Books community. Similar to the Black Study Circle that was advocated by *Black News*, there was no one "teacher" and everyone's voice was of equal value. SOS, like Weusi's column "Around our way," served as the anchoring voices that synthesized the ideas and brought them back to the participants.

The diversity of the POSA format was an invitation for all audience participants to become fully engaged in the event in some way. Active listening, which is to say, the audience was expected to respond if they heard something they were moved by and who showed interest through body language, was always a part of the event. Additionally POSA participants shared and exchanged information, engaged in dialogue about current political issues, or practiced speaking in front of a supportive group. SOS always made it clear that they gave thanks to the "elders" and the "children" and insisted that they were the priority of the day. Once again the urging of bridging the so-called generation gap was one of the main thrusts of the POSA event. In addition to inviting people to read their original poetry, Staajabu and V.S. Chochezi welcomed prose, music, and dance, arguing that this strategy gave participants more agency in defining their experiences. Both mother and daughter believed if the action spoke to you, then that was enough; V.S. Chochezi declared, "if it ignites something, it's good!" Ultimately, Chochezi's beliefs and orientation towards POSA were firmly rooted in her relationship with her mother: "My mother taught me that education is not the responsibility of school. It is the responsibility of the individual. So I was motivated to get my own education and that was instilled in me" (interview, January 10, 2002).

The Straight Out Scribes's organizing strategies for POSA were an extension of the values Staajabu shared with V.S. Chochezi; the value of literacy education was passed on through interpersonal relationships that allowed young people to make decisions about the role reading, writing, and speaking would play in their lives.

"A Whole New World"

An important component in what has been referred to in PLCs as "soldiering" (Fisher 2007b) was being a practitioner of the craft. In other words, the encouragement given to novice writers came from experienced poets, writers, and performers who continued to challenge themselves and to polish their craft. POSA hosts Staajabu and her daughter V.S. Chochezi, always shared their poetry to open and close POSA. Featured poet and writer, Negesti, was also a practitioner who modeled the craft she believed in and fostered. In addition to being a writer, Negesti was teacher, and a midwife. She taught free "Art in the Park" classes in Seattle (after soliciting donations from small business and various organizations).

On one of the days when Negesti was a Carol's Books POSA guest, her reading was particularly special in that some of her former students were in the audience. Sitting in the front row of the poetry reading, Amara Rashad[2] eagerly anticipated hearing her former writing and art teacher share selections from her new book. Amara was the eldest of three children (who were 12, 8, and 6 at the time of the study) of the Rashad family. The Rashad family had home-schooled their daughters and considered POSA to be an extended part of their language arts curriculum, which included making sure that their daughters saw and experienced actual writers and people who enjoyed reading. They consciously sought out POSA for a community to reaffirm literate practices and the "love of language." Extending the experience to their home, the Rashads even created reading events in their home; for example, when each daughter learned to read, they invited family and friends (many of whom they had met at POSA events) to a reading party where each daughter was expected to choose a book or poem to read to the group, and each guest was asked to bring a favorite piece of literature to share.

The Rashads had moved to California from Seattle, Washington. In Seattle, Mrs. Rashad had completed midwifery school and moved with her family to Sacramento where she got a job directing a clinic for pregnant women in need of quality health care. For the Rashad family, home-schooling and consequently participating in POSA were political acts. They believed they could provide their children with a more well-rounded education by tapping into community resources. Like parents involved in the Ocean Hill-Brownsville struggle, the Rashad family sought to create a relevant curriculum for their daughters.

While living in Seattle, the Rashads met Negesti. Born in Richland, Washington, Negesti had been raised in a predominately White community, describing the few Blacks who lived there as "close knit." When she was in high school, an African American couple moved in to her area and became her mentors. Negesti explained that this couple had been knowledgeable about aspects of African American art, literature, and history, and shared their resources with Negesti and other neighbors by hosting classes in their home:

> As I got into high school, there was a couple who moved in the city. I'll never forget them. And they came with Black history. It was during the late sixties, early seventies. They came with all this information and knowledge. I remember [the husband] used to teach these classes and we'd just be sitting there with our mouths open and he asked "Did you know there was a Black National Anthem?" And I ran home and I asked, "Mom, did you know there was a Black National Anthem?" And she started singing it! So I said [to myself] "Wait a minute. If you knew, how come we didn't know?" But it was that movement at that time that you blend in—you become part of the greater whole. And in that we lose ourselves.
>
> (interview, March 30, 2002)

Negesti's discovery that there was a Black National Anthem—and even more startling to her, that her mother *knew* the anthem but never shared it with her—speaks to the experiences of many men and women of her generation whose parents, like her own, felt the importance of "blending in" or assimilating into their white middle-class neighborhood. However, it was these circumstances that inspired Negesti's neighbors to teach classes to young people, and the exposure to this new pool of knowledge pushed Negesti into reading and researching more about people of African descent:

> Just being able to have that eye-opening experience . . . the beauty of it all, I started looking for books. It was just a really wonderful time in my life to discover books and the titles intrigued me; *I am the Darker Brother*, I was like "Wow!" *Black Voices*, "Wow!" You know you start hearing these titles and they were poetic . . . *The Me Nobody Knows, The Invisible Man*. So you

> start looking and searching for more and the more you search
> the more there is. And with those discoveries then other people
> are writing because they're discovering too . . . so it really just
> opened a whole new world to me that I had no idea existed.
>
> (interview, March 30, 2002)

Negesti's admiration of the "Black classics" encouraged her to continue
the search for history through biography and narrative. These were the
same classics Brooks was introduced to by younger poets like Haki
Madhubuti and advertised on the pages of *Black News* simultaneously
challenging European "classics" and questioning the existing literary
canon. In the same way Negesti's neighbors mobilized the young people
of African descent in her suburban community, Negesti became a
community-based teacher as well. Claiming her "small town sista'"
identity, Negesti was committed to remaining in a small city for other
young people who found themselves making similar discoveries. From
1986–1991, Negesti taught at an Independent Black Institution in Seattle
called the Garvey School (named after Marcus Garvey), which offered
"standard learning" such as math, reading, and science, as well as what
she called "our content," or African American perspectives on these
subjects. The Garvey School sought to do what schools like Shule
Jumamose, Uhuru Sasa Shule did—cultivate young Black people to find
their purpose and become literate in a variety of ways. Like her neighbors
who introduced her to new ideas, Negesti recreated opportunities for a
new generation of youth through the Garvey School and free classes she
offered in the city of Seattle. Continuing a tradition of teaching in
grassroots institutions, Negesti created poetry, performance and art
classes (while simultaneously seeking grants for materials and supplies).
Reading at Carol's Books for the POSA series was another way for her to
connect with former students like Amara Rashad, with new young
people, and with their families.

During Negesti's reading, Amara took photographs that she felt were
"important" to the event at Negesti's request. Amara took her job very
seriously; she took pictures from various angles, including from behind
Negesti so that she could capture the audience, as well as from behind
the audience, to capture their perspective of the event. Negesti considered the camera a "representation of commitment" to the young
people she taught and mentored. Negesti also integrated the young
participants by reading her poem, written specifically for her students,

entitled "There are some powerful young writers on this planet earth." In her poem, Negesti depicted her students as capable and responsible participants in their literacy learning. According to Negesti, her students "don't just observe, they participate; they don't just write it, they speak it." Here, Negesti did not dichotomize the oral and written, nor did she isolate literacy learning from action, emphasizing that her students "don't just speak it, they live it; they don't just live it, they be it!" Negesti saw her work with students as returning the "gift" that she had received from her Richland, Washington, neighbor, who had enabled Negesti to experience a teaching and learning space in their home. This experience led to Negesti's eventual quest to read and learn more, and eventually to her passion to "pass on" what she had learned to novice learners. Negesti's poem demonstrated her ability to step back and watch her students take a leadership role in their writing; she observed her students as much as they observed her, and encouraged her audience to do the same: "Give 'em a pen. Watch 'em, watch 'em, watch 'em change the world!" Most importantly, Negesti encouraged her students by demonstrating the very practices she expected from them.

"We're Taking Their Struggle and Passing It On"

Carol's Books POSA and the Jahva House Speak Easy had different formats, yet both took pride in attracting writers with different levels of experiences. Primarily an "open mic" format, the Speak Easy required poets to sign in to read and adhere to the two-poem-maximum rule. Over time, newer poets used the microphone to form relationships with veteran poets by acknowledging their presence and thanking them for their encouragement before they read or performed their original work. The conduit for relationships between members of the community was the Speak Easy host, Greg Bridges, who thought of himself as a "broker" between the various artists who read at the open mic. Bridges was in his forties at the time of the study, straddling the generations of "elders" (who were in their sixties) and "youth" (who were in their early thirties and younger). Although there was no formal assignment of titles, newer poets/activists like NerCity considered more experienced poets such as Sister A an "elder" out of respect and admiration who I will discuss later in this chapter. Serving as "old heads," elders were thought to be knowledgeable not only through formal education, but also through life experiences. Additionally, elders could offer history that helped the community place settings such as the Jahva House Speak Easy in a larger historic, cultural, and artistic context. A poet, musician, teacher and Speak Easy "elder" known as Sister A explained that she experienced places like the Jahva House in New York and that they were a continuum of events that took place during eras such as the Harlem Renaissance:

> Jahva House is just a continuation of what I left in New York. There are always places like this. There always have been places [like this] before I was born. People were doing the same thing before. Langston Hughes, from what I understand, did the same thing in clubs in New York. I remember seeing Eddie Jefferson[3] in a club in New York do something similar. It's a classroom, I learn and hopefully somebody learns from me.
>
> (interview, May 23, 2002)

Comparing Jahva House Speak Easy to a classroom, Sister A noted the reciprocal teaching and learning that takes place of scribes and lovers of words. However, unlike many classrooms, it was not limited to singular notions of literacy, as poetry could be expressed through written text, freestyling, rapping, acoustic instruments, and even dance. Sister A also recognized "there always have been places like this" indicated her sense of her role in a living tradition. Seldom missing a Wednesday night, Sister A liked to come late because she believed the "die hards" would still be there. Sister A also situated spoken word's recent renaissance with the goals and vision of the well-known and highly documented, Langston Hughes and the less-known lyricism of jazz vocalist Eddie Jefferson demonstrating the relationship between spoken word poetry and music. Jefferson, known for his vocalese technique (putting lyrics to established compositions that were originally instrumental), recorded lyrics for famous compositions such as "A Night in Tunisia" and Miles Davis's "So What?" Sister A compared her recollection of Jefferson in a night club in New York as "something similar" to what she experienced in places like the Jahva House Speak Easy that called attention to the many shapes spoken word could take. One of the prevailing attitudes at the Speak Easy was that Black creative expression was a continuum; the blues evolved from work songs, jazz emerged from the blues, and hip hop was close kin to poetry from the Black Arts Movement. This belief was underscored by the deejay who played a mix of music prior to and after the Speak Easy open mic began. This practice was also carried out in Bridges and Sister

A's radio programs, in which one could hear spoken word poetry, blues, hip hop, and jazz from the African Diaspora. Sister A was committed to showing the connection between music traditions such as the blues to spoken word poetry through her own work. In one of her poems that she shared frequently at the Speak Easy, Sister A educated young poets about their connection to blues music, working-class Black people, and the "country" or rural areas of the southern states:

> The blues is as diverse as the people who sing it and those kind of people who are ashamed of [the blues] need to understand there's not one of them whether [they] are from New York . . . Trinidad . . . Canada, not one of us who doesn't have somebody somewhere who didn't pick cotton, chopped cane, picked tobacco or what have you and instead of being ashamed of those people who probably broke their asses so that we could be who we are we should be proud . . . some of them got their hands chopped off so that we could write poetry.
>
> (interview, May 23, 2002)

Sister A's lessons in history at the Speak Easy open mic evolved into a play about the history of the blues in the Bay Area that she wrote and produced. Casting younger poets from the Speak Easy as actors, Sister A encouraged new writers to understand that they were a part of something larger. Other community elders like J. Ali carried similar attitudes about links between generations. Pedagogies of possibility sought to move beyond a superficial understanding of a generation gap; Brooks exemplified this when she reached out to the Blackstone Rangers, the African American Teachers Association reached out to Black youth in Ocean Hill-Brownsville and *Black News* made these young people central to their mission. J. Ali believed that many young people of African descent spent time building oppositional identities because they were not shown how they were linked to other people and important movements:

> I can provide that component of inclusion to let individuals see what they're dealing with is not exclusive to their generation, is not exclusive to a particular time reference. This is something-just like what Quincy [Jones] did with *Back on the Block*. I think when young people have someone that they clearly know

is from a different generation connect with them around issues of art where the young people feel isolated and separated and they now have the opportunity to get a sense that they're part of a continuum. And the extent that they respect and involve themselves in that continuum rather than as being separate, they will also be included and accepted as being part of that continuum as those who are older.

(interview, September 1, 2002)

J. Ali referred to musician-producer Quincy Jones's recording project *Back on the Block*, where Jones invited young musicians to collaborate with him and more experienced musicians. Jones, who began his career as a jazz musician, played with many jazz legends and was able to reconnect with the hip hop generation with his launching of Vibe magazine. Jones created opportunities for newer musicians and artists to get work as writers and performers. Extending a folk saying "I've been around the block and back" or "I've already experienced what you have and more," Jones wanted to show young people that he could participate in their new traditions and vice versa. J. Ali saw Jones's work as a roadmap for how to teach younger people about the history of art forms and forms of expression without isolating them or degrading their efforts to create something new.

Younger generations in the Speak Easy accepted the responsibility of continuing a tradition crafting words with pride and purpose. NerCity and his poetry partner, Scorpio Blues, began their own spoken word venue as a result of their experiences at the Speak Easy and with its predecessor Dorsey's Locker.[4] NerCity also saw himself and other poets in their twenties and thirties as vehicles to get school-aged students involved. NerCity enjoyed receiving recognition from his peers but he also valued getting the feedback from more experienced artists and audience participants like Sister A and J. Ali:

That's one of the greatest things in the world to have someone much older than you, who's been to more places than you to say "you know what, young man, I enjoyed your work." Sister A came to Dorsey's one time and she just said these pieces that blew my mind back. She loved my pieces and she called me "son" the first night. It's a great thing to have the elders in there because we're taking their struggle and we're passing it on. And

I'm just holding it for a little while so the youngsters can get it. [There are] so many generations in this forum, when you're doing spoken word you're saying how you feel and still put it in a form that you are in a way of hip hop but you are doing the spoken word and respected. It's the greatest feeling in the world. And I feel that a lot of [elders] passed that torch and they feel comfortable passing that torch to [me and Scorpio Blues] because we are not going to drop it.

(interview, May 23, 2002)

Emphasizing mutual respect and a serious commitment to be active in each others' lives, the many generations at the Speak Easy continuously nurtured each other. NerCity's statement traces one of the sources of motivation triggered by these interpersonal relationships with elder soldiers at the Speak Easy. Both NerCity and Blues started attending the events as observers. Once they became comfortable, they began to read their work on the mic. With the encouragement of hosts like Greg Bridges and veteran poets, NerCity and Blues began to perform and eventually host their own events (Fisher 2005a). First, NerCity raised the issue of his writing and performance being acknowledged, recognized, and respected by an experienced writer. Second, NerCity understood this acknowledgement to be part of the larger responsibility to "taking their struggle and passing it on." NerCity and Scorpio Blues composed poetry that critically examined the words and actions of their peers while remaining accessible to elders and youth. On a night that the Speak Easy was going to be aired on a local television station, both poets chose pieces that they hoped would reach a wider audience beyond the venue.

In his poem "Me/He/She/We," NerCity began with a critique of people referring to themselves and others as "niggas." Eventually, he revealed that the people talking were not of African descent by asking "Don't you hate it when people talk like that? Especially when they aren't even Black?" At this point, NerCity contrasted what he believed were media-generated stereotypes of blackness with what being Black meant for him:

This is for all those suburban faces
trying to act like those urban races
See I don't want my own people to be niggas
So why would I want you to be niggas . . .

See if you want to emulate me why don't you emulate 300 of us
    getting stacked on boats coming over here
See, that's me
While she was getting raped by master
While he was getting beat by master
And me, I couldn't do nothing 'cause master had all of us
    shackled down
Locked down
See, that's me
See, you don't want to be me . . .
You know what's me?
Muhammad Ali not going to Vietnam.
That's me
The 1968 Olympics
Best believe that's me
[Sister A (with her fist in the air): That's right!]
[NerCity (acknowledging Sister A): Put that fist in the air.]
[Greg Bridges: Word.]
That's me.
My father going to work everyday
That's me
Us getting together in this environment
That's we/me/he/she
Not these wannabees

Aligning his identity with particular moments in African American history, NerCity asserted that if someone wanted to emulate him or Black people in general, they would first have to understand the physical and psychological terror of the enslavement of Africans in the Americas. NerCity held up athlete and activist Muhammad Ali's refusal to enter the military draft as well as the Black athletes in the 1968 Olympics as examples of courage in the face of critique. These references provoked feedback from both Sister A and Greg Bridges, who were listening attentively from the audience. In the closing of his poem, NerCity posited that the daily lives of men like his father who worked every day and the members of the Speak Easy community were ultimate role models.

    Explaining to the guest host from the television station that her writing was largely inspired by elders like her grandmother, Scorpio

Blues went next, and shared her piece about reclaiming womanhood which began with a song:[5]

When I wake to greet the day
I give thanks and then shake the hate
I got a whole world to face
I've been trying to hold it down
'Though sometimes I feel like breaking down
But I gotta' keep moving
(Several people in the audience can be heard shouting "Yeah,
   keep moving girl")
The world won't wait for you
So you gotta do what you came to do
'Cause nobody's going to hold your hand
Nobody's going to prove your plan, only you can
I am what I am and what I am is a woman
Hey y'all
Hey y'all
I am what I am and what I am is a woman
Hey y'all
Hey y'all

Today I was reincarnated as a woman
A month ago I was a ho
Two weeks ago I was a trick
Last week I was a broad
And yesterday I was a bitch
But today
Today I was reincarnated as a woman

Taking back my name
Putting it back on my desk
Taking back my birthright
And letting it shine across my chest
I am claiming once again what should have never been left
Having you know there is a knowledge of mind that goes along
   with these breasts
I'm talking about the same name that day to day gets stripped
   from me
And I find myself having to fight for it

> Both emotionally and physically
> I mean I do my best to spread positivity
> But there's only so much of it left in me
> Because I'm constantly being weakened by words of men
> Who try to tear down my identity . . .

Scorpio Blues captivated the crowd every time she shared this piece. Her desire to increase the visibility of this poem was motivated by her disdain for media images that continuously denigrated women, and Black women in particular. Tracing the evolution of degrading names used against women, Scorpio Blues reclaimed the title "woman" in her refrain throughout the poem.[6] She and NerCity had similar goals for their poetry: They hoped to be catalysts for linking older with new generations. On days of Greg Bridges's rare absence, NerCity hosted the Speak Easy. She also co-organized an open mic with Scorpio Blues on a different night of the week than Speak Easy nights. Eventually, with the support of the Speak Easy family, NerCity and Scorpio Blues moved to Sister A's hometown, New York City, to continue their commitment to spoken word. Not only did they perform in venues throughout the city, but they also became involved with the teen spoken word program Urban Word and hosted one of the 6th annual preliminary slam competitions at the Apollo Theater in Harlem. Sister A believed that young people like NerCity and Scorpio Blues should be given credit for preserving certain aspects of Black education and culture:

> And then usually it's some grandchild who finally realizes "Oh my God" and he'll snatch it back. For whatever reasons grand-children and grandparents always have gotten real tight and that's how spoken word has come back. Like right now you'll hear the hip hop songs and they'll have pieces that are taken from Curtis Mayfield and James Brown. So you'll hear some of the stuff in there and that's how it comes around when young people get sick of all this self-hatred so they pick it up and turn it around.
>
> (interview, May 23, 2002)

Sister A's choice of the linguistic device "snatch it back" helped her to signify an historic cycle that included a reclamation of culture, history, and tradition around expression. Sister A's understanding of this cycle reflects the critical step of "becoming" the writer, reader and speaker that evolves through the relationships which she believed "skipped" a generation. The sampling in hip hop music was a strategy, according to Sister A, that young people used as part of reclaiming. Embedded in this movement to seek elements of one's culture, according to Sister A, was a deliberate refusal to accept negative imagery that has possibly led young people of African descent to not accept themselves as participants in literary communities. NerCity and Scorpio Blues were those "grand-children" who refused to be limited by self-hatred and stereotypes.

"Blood Is Running Between These Lines": Sustaining Current Literate and Literary Communities

Michael Datcher, a poet and author of a national bestselling memoir *Raising Fences: A Black Man's Love Story* from Los Angeles, California, and Gabrilla Ballard, a poet, songwriter and musician from New Orleans, Louisiana, participated in both spoken word poetry open mic events at the Jahva House Café "Speak Easy" and "Mahogany" at the Jamaica House. Additionally, Datcher did readings for *Raising Fences* at both Marcus Books and Carol's Books. Writing workshops and collectives in addition to open mic events for expressionists like Datcher and Ballard have become a way for many writers of Black to share their work and get constructive feedback. These forums bring together oral, aural, and written traditions; the formats for the writing workshops generally include time for interacting with the text in addition to sharing the work aloud. "Open mic" events welcome all forms of expression such as poetry, singing, rapping and sometimes dance; one of the prevailing understandings is that there will be a predominantly Black (African American, African, and Caribbean) audience and much like *Black News*, people are encouraged to "tell it like it is" (see Chapter 3). Although I met Datcher and Ballard at the venues in my study, I learned that their participation evolved from previous experiences in similar PLCs in other cities. Two collaborative reading/writing/performing groups were part of the foundation for Datcher and Ballard's foundation as writers; the Anansi Writers' Workshop at the World Stage in Los Angeles and the *NOMMO* Literary Society in New Orleans respectively. Both Datcher and Ballard noted these two institutions as being critical to their development as writers and expressionists through rituals of perform-ance, practice and feedback that helped them build confidence.

In a section of South Central Los Angeles lies the "village" of Leimert Park. This village is home to many Black businesses including a performance space called the World Stage. Serving as an intersection for jazz musicians, poets, and writers, the World Stage was established in 1992 by the late jazz drummer Billy Higgins and poet Kamau Daáood. In *Raising Fences*, Datcher recounts his first encounter with Daáood in a chapter simply titled "World Stage." Datcher had been conducting a writing workshop for performance poets in his home and learned of the Anansi Writers' Workshop. Datcher wanted to revive the workshop and went to Leimert Park to introduce himself to Daáood and discuss this possibility. Daáood explained to Datcher in a scene from this chapter that the World Stage was a "sacred space" as if to forewarn Datcher about what he was getting himself into. Although he does not go into details in the text, it becomes clear that Daáood trusted Datcher to carry on this important tradition. Daáood passed the workshop to Datcher like Brooks passed her workshop with the Blackstone Rangers to a younger Walter Bradford underscoring the need for "adult initiators" to step back and make room for the future. The writing workshop at the World Stage took place before the open mic event that Datcher hosted the same evening creating a culture of 'workshopping" pieces before poets got to the mic. Datcher, who was in his early thirties at the time of our interview, explained to me that he had to learn about the history of the World Stage and the musicians and poets who became the pillars of this community. This community also nurtured creativity, and institutions building among its participants. Elders like Daáood and Higgins passed this history on to poets like Datcher who continued to foster this spirit among their peers:

> Artists come in a very serious way and [with] much respect and much love I should say as well—and provide very healthy feedback. We encourage you to keep in mind that their blood is running between these lines . . . [the Anansi Writing Workshop] is so dynamic, so alive, and people are thinking and readers are getting really incredible feedback.
>
> (interview, March 26, 2002)

Datcher's inclusion of the World Stage in his memoir marked an important time in his personal development where he began to be critical about his own writing. In *Raising Fences*, Datcher noted that those who "workshopped" their poems often became the most appreciated poets on the mic:

> There is no sign-up list for the workshop segment. The first person to bound onstage in front of the mic gets to read and receive feedback. After two years of being involved, I realize that the poets who workshop the most have become the best poets. As a result, the workshop section has become extremely popular. Poets who plan to receive feedback arrive early and cluster in the front-row seats. As soon as the person onstage finishes and steps one foot off the stage, the would-be-next workshoppers aggressively jump on. If it's close the crowd determines who was first. This good-natured ritual sends the message that while others flee from constructive criticism, the World Stage poets are hungry to get better.
>
> (2001, p. 203)

The ritual of racing to the stage and the mic at the workshop showed the passion and eagerness these writers expressed for developing both writing and performance skills. Writers were dedicated to both spoken and written words and did not spend time assigning a hierarchy to either. The mic and stage were an extension of the journal and pen. Datcher emphasized that the workshop attracted a "full range" of the Black community "across economic lines and across ideology." At the time of our interview, the Anansi Writers' Workshop proudly claimed six published books by participants.[7] In fact, Datcher credited the writing of his memoir to his participation in an open mic culture because he considered his bestselling memoir to be a "long poem." When addressing Black bookstore audiences, Datcher took time to talk about his memoir in relationship to Blues traditions in African American music. Datcher described the Blues tradition as growing out of "Blacks being captured as prisoners of war from Africa and brought to America and enslaved."[8] In addition to evolving from the Blues tradition, Datcher considered his writing to also a direct descendant of jazz music. Jazz trumpeter, Miles Davis, was as influential to Datcher's writing as the poets and writers with whom he shared the World Stage. Since the World Stage was both a jazz performance space as well as home to a writing workshop and open mic event, both musicians and poets saw each other as essential to their evolution as artists. This, too, was seen in the pages of *Black News* who dedicated advertising to literature, theatre, and music. During his composition process, Datcher said he listened to Miles Davis's famous album "Kind of Blue" which Datcher considers a "collage of Blackness" or stories that came from multiple experiences of being Black in the context of the United States.

Raising Fences chronicled Datcher's life growing up in South Central Los Angeles with a hard working single mother and a life of yearning for "picket fence dreams" which Datcher described as "a played-out metaphor in the white community but one still secretly riding the bench in black neighborhoods nationwide" (p. 3). Through his participation in the writing workshop and confronting issues in his own life, Datcher developed the courage to tell his story. Through the merging of music, poetry and prose Datcher carved *Raising Fences*:

> It's just me trying to tell my hard luck life in a way that is artistic. I'm a poet so I really believe in the power of language. I can work it, twist it, turn it and kind of meld it into patterned tapestry. So I wanted to tell the story with a certain level of linguistic delicacy . . . so you would recognize the people in these stories, the voices that were talking to you in this book. You recognize the rhythm.
> (interview, March 26, 2002)

Datcher also saw his memoir as being a way to convey that men of African descent were both "human and beautiful." Much like members of the literary societies documented by McHenry who saw their engagement with literature as demonstrating to their former enslavers that they were not inferior, Datcher viewed writing as a way for Black people to earn respect from the world. Additionally, Datcher also believed that having a facility with words both spoken and written was critical and open mics and Black bookstores were an important part of fostering this skill:

> If you can use the language in a way that is interesting, different and powerful, people will respect that. For a business to deal in the production of Black creation, of Black imagination is beautiful, and it's a symbol of hope. Because with education comes the opportunity to advance in life and to uplift the race if you would.
> (interview, March 26, 2002)

Like Datcher, I met Gabrilla Ballard through the sites in my study. She was 23 at the time of the study and new to the Northern California poetry scene. However, she was familiar with similar networks in her native New Orleans, Louisiana. Relocating to California to do work in education reform, Ballard sought the Jahva House "Speak Easy" open mic event because she wanted to establish herself in a community of Black expressionists who were also community activists. Ballard considered many of her poem/songs to be messages to people of African descent. The first night I heard Ballard, she performed a poem/song entitled "Are you ready?" while playing an acoustic guitar:

Are you ready
to stop living the lie?
Are you ready
to open your eyes?
Are you ready
to give up your life?
Are you ready?

By the end of the piece, Ballard strategically changed the "you" to "we" and invited the open mic community to participate using the call and response format. Ballard later explained in an interview that she wrote this piece with people of African descent in mind:

When I say [in the song] "we build up walls-this ain't us" I mean that historically and even now in certain areas of the world we are connected. We are a community and we take care of each other. I think sometimes we are so concerned about being hurt or failing in others' eyes that we don't even try . . . if you mess up, okay you messed up but at least you tried!

(interview, May 14, 2002)

Because she worked with elementary school-aged students in urban settings, Ballard's work was sometimes influenced by her efforts to help them see their own value and talents. Ballard believed that her own self-confidence emerged as not only a writer and a reader but also a performer. During our interview, Ballard explained that her experience in a youth-centered church that encouraged her to write, direct and perform plays in addition to her participation in an African-centered school and eventually her membership in a collective of writers, readers and speakers called the *NOMMO* Literary Society were her foundation for being engaged in literacy practices.[9] In her church, Ballard and the youth in the congregation were often asked to write plays about different issues in their communities. Ballard fondly remembered writing and directing a play about drugs in the community; "my spirit was nurtured in speaking up against injustice . . . when properly nurtured children can do anything. Who knows what they grow up to be!" Both Ahidiana and the *NOMMO* Literary Society were part of the work that poet, writer, historian and teacher Kalamu ya Salaam did in the New Orleans area. Salaam, a native of New Orleans, is to New Orleans who Weusi is to Brooklyn. Salaam and other colleagues co-founded an Independent Black Institution, Ahidiana Work Study Center, which exhibited similar value systems as Uhuru Sasa out of the EAST:

> Ahidiana was a school that was based in African, African American culture. It [was] an independent school and the curriculum was structured by the teachers but it was very holistic. It was hands on; it taught us to have love, respect and just honor for who we are as Africans—Diasporic Africans. You know that's important because many of [the teachers] had Pan-Africanist views. We didn't feel separate from the continent, you know what I mean? And some people argue that the school prepared us for a world that doesn't exist. I don't agree with that. I feel that the school created—prepared us to create the world that we wanted to exist because what other reason are we teaching anyway?
>
> (interview, May 14, 2002)

Ahidiana, according to Salaam, promoted "self-determination" and shunned competition with the understanding that "everyone helped each other" (interview, April 2, 2002). Like Brooks and Weusi, Salaam's parents encouraged reading and education. Salaam's mother taught in New Orleans public schools and Salaam attended the schools where his mother taught. Through Ahidiana, Salaam introduced Ballard to a value system in education where students were able to be active in their learning process; she said teachers consistently consulted students about projects and what they wanted to contribute to the learning community. Ballard's love for reading, writing, and performing were only beginning to be cultivated at this time. Salaam would continue to serve as her mentor and eventually be the first to publish one of her poems. Salaam heard Ballard perform her poem "When Daddy Died" about the loss of her father at 15 years old; Salaam helped her edit the poem and Ballard explained "from that point on" she continued to write and became a member of the *NOMMO* Literary Society.[10]

Established in New Orleans in 1995, the *NOMMO* Literary Society was a group of writers with a range of ages and life experiences who met weekly. During the weekly meetings, members of the society completed a common reading, shared an original composition, and exchanged feedback. Salaam fostered the talents of poets and writers in New Orleans in the same way Daáood did in Los Angeles. On the second Friday of every month, the *NOMMO* held a public reading at the Community Book Center, a Black bookstore also located in New Orleans.[11] The physical space of the *NOMMO* Literary Society had countless shelves of books written by and about people of African descent throughout the world. Aesthetically the space was beautiful; there was a spiral staircase, two fireplaces, and tables and chairs so that people could make themselves at home. In addition to books, Salaam provided the society with a comprehensive collection of music including jazz, blues and other forms of Black music. Jazz musicians like Coltrane had multiple drawers dedicated to their work while writers like Amiri Baraka and Langston Hughes had their own bookshelves. It was in this context that Ballard and other writers sharpened their skills as readers, writers, and participants in space that valued knowledge. All of these materials were available to members of the *NOMMO* group.

Both Datcher and Ballard understood their writing to be part of a larger continuum of literate and literary practices for people of African descent. For example, Ballard saw the *NOMMO* and the open mics as part of the same tradition as her church, Ahidiana, and *NOMMO*. These institutions helped Ballard develop a writing identity grounded not only in poetry and prose but also music and performance. Similarly, Datcher saw his foundation as a poet based in blues and jazz music traditions as a foundation to writing his memoir. Datcher and Ballard believed that having community-based role models such as Daáood and Salaam as critical to their development as writers; these mentors were not only poets and writers but also activists and historians in their communities. Institutions like the World Stage and *NOMMO* as well as the venues in which I observed both Datcher and Ballard were committed to emerging writers and supporting their development.

360 Degrees

During an interview I conducted as part of the larger study with scholar and educator, Wade Nobles,[12] I asked him if he believed that the readers, writers, speakers and "doers" who are visible in the spoken word poetry venues and bookstore events in my study have come full circle. We had just attended a reading for Ilyasah Shabazz , the middle daughter of the late Dr. Betty Shabazz and Malcolm X at Marcus Books in Oakland, California. The reading attracted not only people from Dr. Shabazz's and Malcolm X's generation like Dr. Nobles but also the peers of Ilyasah Shabazz. Dr. Nobles explained "I don't know if the circle's coming back around . . . I think that the song is unfinished . . . it's still unfolding" (June 16, 2002). Indeed, the "song is unfinished" and "unfolding" in Participatory literacy communities, anthologies, self-published books, and recordings. However, as the title of Kalamu ya Salaam and Kwame Alexander's anthology *360° A Revolution of Black Poets*, suggests there is an acknowledgment that the up and coming Black writers are well-aware of the poets, writers, musicians, performers, and institutions of the word from past literary movements. They have not simply stopped at becoming aware; they, too, are establishing institutions including new venues and events as well as producing publications and recorded performances. So what is "new" about the "new literate and literary" and what has remained the same? Participants in this recent renaissance of open mics, writing groups and published work are determined, much like their predecessors, to maintain literacy communities where they can access reading, writing, discussion and debates through poetry, prose and other forms of expression.

Another similarity is that the venues in which these events are held often serve multiple functions. When examining organizations like the EAST, the World Stage, and the *NOMMO* Literary Society, it is evident that their founders and organizers tried to create a home for all forms of Black expression with a firm grounding in literacy. For example the Jahva House Speak Easy open mic where I first met and heard Datcher and Ballard was a café that was transformed into a cultural center in the evening. Owners of these establishments share their space with the community and organize events that meet the needs of people of African descent. This outreach is an extension of the sense of responsibility that evolved from the "chain letter of instruction" or passing on knowledge and information as seen in the outreach of Gwendolyn Brooks in the same spirit as IBIs of the 1960s and 1970s from which *Black News* emerged. Part of passing on knowledge and information for the literate and literary of African descent was making the word accessible in print through oral presentation. The Anansi Writers' Workshop at the World Stage and the *NOMMO* Literary Society incorporated time for writing, revising and also sharing the work orally; there is an understanding that words were not solely for display but to incite action.

There has also been a shift in the make up of the communities McHenry and Heath examined and the current practitioners of the word. I use the term "shift" because I view these communities as part of a continuum which does not lend itself to dichotomizing terms such as "contrast." Current practitioners of the word cut across socio-economic lines. Ballard considered this to be one of the most important aspects of the open mic communities:

> It's just a mix of all kinds of us. It's like people who are educated—formally educated or institutionally educated. Then there are people who are self-educated . . . just from every class background you can think of. We are there . . . Come as you are.
>
> (May 14, 2002)

Ballard's church-inspired "come as you are" has become a value in the open mic spaces. There are other shifts in the continuum of the literate and literary of African descent; one of the most compelling is that while newer poets and writers in theory have access to the institutions that the readers and writers of the nineteenth century did not, they are still organizing spaces as both "supplementary" and "alternative" institutions by choice (Fisher, 2006a). This was also evident during the Black Arts Movement and the rise of IBIs. One reason for this may be that despite access to these formal institutions, there is still a pervasive lack of recognition of new forms of poetry, writing and thinking about language. This quest for supplemental knowledge in addition to methods is one that draws Black expressionists to these spaces. Part of that is the role of music; Poets and writers like Datcher and Ballard understand Black music traditions such as the Blues, jazz and hip hop as being inspiration for the writing process. This is evident in the fact that Ballard can play her guitar at an open mic and it is still considered poetry. The inclusion of deejays at the open mic events is another example of the importance of music. Leimert Park's World Stage is a home to both jazz musicians and poets while the *NOMMO* Literary Society had as many music recordings available to its members as it did books and periodicals. It is not even an issue among participants; music is simply a part of the fabric of these spaces. And finally, to some degree there is still a belief that literacy is linked to freedom; however the freedom does not come from acquiring skills often associated with literacy or even mastering literary texts. The freedom now is in the ability to use words to challenge and critique as well as to motivate and inspire newer generations of readers, writers and speakers. With the sense of history, novice writers, readers and speakers can create their own space in this historical continuum. Teaching literature and literacy for young people should involve the teaching of history as well as integrate the current movement of expressionists. This is evidenced by programs by the work of poet teachers such as Kalamu ya Salaam with Students at the Center in New Orleans and Joseph Ubiles with Power Writing in New York City (Buras, forthcoming; Fisher, 2005a, 2005b, 2007a). Both programs, which work with youth of color, draw from the poet/activist traditions inspired by the Black Arts Movement in which both Salaam and Ubiles were active.

The common thread throughout all of these communities and spaces across time is the belief that words incite action. Written words are not merely for the pages of books sitting on shelves but to be whispered, spoken, or shouted as well as exchanged, discussed, debated and used to organize and inspire. These communities have much to teach the education world about how to create a climate for literacy teaching and learning. How can the practices in these communities inform the way we think about how reading, writing, and orality are taught? PLCs force teachers, teacher educators in schools and in out-of-school contexts to rethink the relationship between history and language arts as well as how creating forums and "open mics" support democratic engagement. Pedagogies of possibility found in Brooks's work, on the pages of *Black News* and in the bookstores and spoken word poetry venues are not only embedded in the actual poetry and writings but the ways in which these practices are carried out. The practices found in PLCs are not limited to out-of-school communities; literacy activists and advocates have found their way to some public school classrooms.

CHAPTER 5

Catching the Fire

Black Teachers as Literacy Activists in Urban Public Schools

"You are the author of your own life story" read a brightly colored banner that greeted students, teachers, and visitors in the foyer of Benjamin Banneker Academy for Community Development in the Clinton Hill section of Brooklyn, New York. Flags representing Barbados, Brazil, Cuba, Nigeria, and countless other countries in the African Diaspora were suspended from the ceiling creating a sea of vivid colors and patterns. In an enclosed case displaying the names of the school and district administrators read yet another quotation: "Our children may learn about the heroes of the past . . . Our task is to make ourselves architects of the future."[1] I had an appointment to meet the literacy coach, Cathie Wright-Lewis or "Mama C," but I arrived to Benjamin Banneker in the middle of passing period and got caught in the whirlwind of students rushing from one class to another. A sea of faces, all of brown hues, briefly filled the foyer and adjacent hallways before quickly disappearing into classrooms. Mama C and I had already talked for hours on the phone prior to meeting about her teaching philosophy, politics, and the possibility of me visiting her "spoken wordologists."

A product of "resegregation" or a "resegregated society" (Alim, 2005), approximately 89.2 percent of Benjamin Banneker's (Banneker) 670 students identified themselves as "Black/African American" during the 2003–2004 academic year. Later, Mama C told me that Banneker was originally slated to be a school for African American male students only. However, when this exclusively male student configuration was beginning to stir controversy the school promptly enrolled female students as well. Mama C, a native daughter of the Ocean Hill-Brownsville section of Brooklyn, attended segregated schools some thirty years prior to entering the teaching force only to find herself in segregated schools once again. As a "literacy coach," Mama C was responsible for working with all content-area teachers on implementing reading and writing in meaningful ways across the curriculum. She conducted professional development workshops, helped organize the Writing Center at Banneker, and started the after-school spoken word poetry club.

The aim of this chapter is to illustrate how the values of literacy activism found in the writing workshops of poets and writers like Gwendolyn Brooks, in the pages of *Black News*, and in Independent Black Institutions established in the late 1960s and early 1970s, and more recently in the form of Black bookstores and open mic events have been adapted by Black teachers in urban public schools. Using the lens of "Critical Studyin'" in literacy (King, 2006), I analyze the literacy practices of Mama C and her student poets who were "studyin' freedom" in an after-school poetry community (Fisher, 2005, 2006). "Studyin' freedom" or Critical Studyin',' according to King, is part of a larger tradition of Citizenship Schools and the Freedom Schools of the Civil Rights Movement. Evoking the literacy learning of Frederick Douglass as a framework for understanding African American education, King contends the "hope" and eventual power of reading, writing, and orality gave Douglass fuel to struggle for his freedom and eventually freedom of others (King, 2006, p. 355). Much like the "chain letter of instruction" (Holt, 1990, p. 94) discussed in Chapter 1, enslaved Africans pieced together literate identities by exercising the value of reciprocity:

> Just as Blacks maintained an invisible church, separate from the ones whites provided for them, they also maintained secret schools. These schools could be found in every major southern city and in countless rural communities and plantations. Their teachers were often barely literate themselves, but they passed on what little they knew to others in what one may call a chain letter of instruction.
>
> (p. 94)

It is in this same spirit that teachers like Mama C have created networks within the framework of public schools. Although Mama C's group was not a "secret," she impressed upon the young writers in this group that it was their responsibility to share and exchange knowledge and information with their peers and communities. The "Spoken Wordologists," as Mama C called them, included 9th, 10th, 11th, and 12th graders. Sister T, an English teacher at Banneker, volunteered her classroom for the meetings and participated in the circle. In order to introduce the concept to the school Mama C piloted a spoken word class with 12th graders who had fulfilled their Regents requirements but who were still unsure of their lives beyond high school. Mama C was a Sojourner Truth of sorts—leading students to freedom—freedom to know one's history, freedom of speech and creativity while providing opportunities for students to "develop more complete historical knowledge, critical thinking skills, and self-knowledge" (King, 2006, p. 345).

In Mama C's spoken word poetry class, student poets were "Critical Studyin'" in an effort to re-educate themselves much like the efforts of *Black News* about contemporary portrayals of African Americans engaged in civil rights struggles as well as the histories of enslaved Africans in the Americas. During the 2003–2004 academic year, I volunteered in the Writing Center at Banneker and I was a participant observer in Mama C's spoken word poetry class. Using qualitative methods including participant observation, ethnographic field notes, ethnographic video, and interviews with Mama C and her students, I wanted to understand how Mama C's class was part of a phenomenon of teachers implementing out-of-school literacy practices and elements of youth cultural productions such as spoken word in school contexts. I discovered there was a strong history and social studies presence in addition to Language Arts in Mama C's curriculum. It became evident that Mama C was not merely implementing out-of-school practices but grounding her pedagogy in a larger philosophy of African American education in which literacy was central. Ultimately Mama C's objective was to cultivate a new generation of readers, writers, thinkers as well as "doers" by guiding them on a journey through American and World History. Student poets were encouraged to link their lived experiences with the histories of Black people locally, nationally, and globally.

"Heroes Nobody Has Heard Of": Mama C and the "Runaway Slaves of the 21st Century"

Born in 1958, Mama C grew up in the Brownsville section of Brooklyn where she would see her neighbors engaged in a fight for community control of public schools. When asked about Brownsville, Mama C launched into a discussion about the overwhelming number of housing projects, "When you visit Brownsville you see more housing projects than anywhere else. Some go as high as 17 floors, some 21." In the early 1900s, Harlem and Bedford-Stuyvesant were the primary neighborhoods for Blacks in New York. Brownsville began to attract the African American working class and many of whom had been "almost completely excluded from New York's industrial economy" (Pritchett, 2002, p. 41). Black families still found ways to make a living and their numbers in the Brownsville section of Brooklyn began to increase significantly. Housing, according to Pritchett, was a concern in Brownsville as early as the 1920s when housing that was "built quickly and cheaply . . . resulted in serious sanitation and health problems" (p. 47). Pritchett contends that public housing continued to have a large presence in Brownsville in the late 1980s and early 1990s with a reported 21,302 residents living in New York City Housing Authority buildings. Mama C noted that although she was aware that housing projects are considered synonymous to crime and poverty, there was a time when she felt safe in her public housing community: "Before the drug trafficking became a major disruption and corruption in the neighborhood it was a loving place for children. It was kid city . . . everywhere you turned there were kids. You couldn't help but have a friend." (interview, February 20, 2004).

Mama C referred to the Brownsville section as "the edge of the city" as did many of her peers while she was growing up. Her mother, a young divorcee who struggled to raise her five children, eventually began a career in teaching and would later encourage Mama C to do the same. Mama C believed it was almost standard for Black children like herself, her siblings, and her peers to have a limited understanding of their heritage. She further believed that her mis-education as a student in urban public schools perpetuated this lack of knowledge:

> Until I was ten years old, I thought the only history we had was that we were slaves in America. This is all I had heard and all I knew, "Our people were slaves. Our people were separated. The

master raped us. We're doomed to die because slavery is always going to exist in some shape or form and that's why we live in the ghetto and why we are poor and that's how life is going to be."

(interview, February, 20, 2004)

In the late 1960s and early 1970s, young members of the Black Panther Party and other activists such as Jitu Weusi were becoming more visible Mama C's community; they were organizing programs and generating resources among children in urban neighborhoods like Brownsville throughout the United States. After she turned 10, Mama C's mother allowed her to participate in a summer programs organized by young Panthers as well as the EAST's Uhuru Sasa Shule:

Brownsville was one of the areas where young Panthers and new revolutionaries came to help the neighborhood and uplift the children. So I was one of those kids. And some of [the teachers] were no older than ten years older than I but they were conscious and they wore afros and they wore red, black, and green. We had an African history class, a Black history class and [the teacher] told us that our ancestors had been kings and queens. We were like "What? I never heard that before." I always thought I was poor little colored, welfare, bastard child. That's all I ever thought I was. It shook me.

(interview, February 20, 2004)

Similar to Negesti's experience in the suburbs of Seattle, these were Black men and women who were "soldiers"—that is, they were committed to organizing learning communities for Black youth (Fisher, 2007b). Although Mama C was too young to be completely involved in the Ocean Hill-Brownsville struggle she remembers this chaotic time in her neighborhood and the inevitability of change. She could not name the changes she was witnessing at that time but these "new Blacks," to borrow Brooks's words, were in her community and she admired them and what they had to say. Mama C was profoundly influenced by summer programs in the spirit of the EAST's Uhuru Sasa Shule:

And the more they talked about what happened through slavery—of course all the pictures in my mind were the ones fed to society of the happy slaves, singing and dancing—they blew [my image] up right then and there. [The teachers] told us the truth right then and there . . . They told us what the real deal was. They told us about the rebellious Nat Turner who became my hero. I mean I fell in love with Sojourner Truth. I did not know any of this. It shaped me. It became my foundation. And they also made us pledge and promise that we would always teach our history.

(interview, February 20, 2004)

More than anything Mama C remembers being encouraged to read. Her new teachers did not want her to merely take their words for it; they wanted her to conduct her own research and do her own reading. When I met Mama C in 2003, she had been teaching in New York City for 20 years. Prior to teaching she considered a career in law and took a job with the New York Police Department (NYPD) as a 911 operator while studying for the LSAT. With a newly minted degree in English, Mama C was an avid writer and working for NYPD never stopped that. She wrote everywhere and on any piece of paper she could find. Mama C wrote plays, poems, and some short stories:

I was a police dispatcher for 911 . . . and the school [where my mother] was had a lot of problems . . . I told her, "Look you need to get out of there because I'm sending cars there everyday." [My mother] said, "Don't worry, this principal is going to turn it all upside down. I want you to meet him, you would like his politics. He's all about the community, Cathie. You gotta' meet him." And that's how she got me.

(interview, February 20, 2004)

This principal who was going to "turn it all upside down" happened to be Frank Mickens and Mama C did not realize it but after she returned to school and completed her education credits, she would work for Mickens for approximately 14 years before joining the Banneker staff. Mickens, who Mama C refers to as "homeboy from Bed-Stuy who was well-loved and respected," recognized Mama C's passion for music and literature. According to Mama C, Mickens "hooked" her when he told her she would have full access to the auditorium and the stage for her teaching. The irony of Mama C's change in career from a 911 Operator to a teacher was that she was "part of the mission" that turned the school where she was sending police cars and the fire department personnel to as a 911 operator "upside down." The ideology that guided her teaching as well as Mickens's mentoring was not at all unlike what she experienced in her summer programs with revolutionaries, Black Panthers and Uhuru Sasa:

> I've always brought my whole self to the classroom . . . Mickens was just like that and made sure teachers were giving beyond. You don't just come to teach a subject. You bring your heart and soul. You bring who you are.
>
> (interview, February 20, 2004)

These values were central to the argument *Black News* tried to make throughout its tenure to Black youth, their parents, and Black educators. Education and learning was an around the clock process. When Mama C began the work at Banneker, she continued to make herself available beyond the traditional school hours. I learned about Mama C's ongoing commitment to young people in our first meeting when she gave me a copy of her novel, *Mauraya's Seed—Why hope lives behind project walls*, which she had recently published. *Mauraya's Seed* told the story of a young woman named Passion who was struggling to raise her children in "Browns' Village" during the height of the Civil Rights and eventually Black Power Movements. After her husband, Justice, returned home from the Vietnam War and was killed in Brownsville's streets fighting against drug trafficking, Passion became focused on her children's education. As one of the only parents daring enough to allow her children to be bused to an all-white school in another neighborhood, Passion worked hard to supplement her children's public school education with Black and African history and culture in order to build their self-confidence. In one scene Passion noticed that things were changing in her community, "The people of the community were becoming conscious and it showed in the way they dressed, the way they walked, and the way they talked. Common conversation was almost always political, which was exactly what Justice wanted" (Wright-Lewis, 2001, p. 152). Mama C, who considered herself a Brownsville griot, created characters who reflected her own experiences watching her neighbors become more political during the Ocean Hill-Brownsville struggle for community control. Passion and other characters in the novel also demonstrated a growing sense of history in the same way Mama C experienced after being exposed to community programs as a young person:

> Cultural exchanges occurred during holidays and seasonal festivals in a way that never had before. Sharing of information rediscovered since and before the Harlem Renaissance was discussed. History from indigenous people who hadn't lost the ways of the elders and ancestors were reintegrated into the lifestyle of the new inner-city African American natives. Words of Negro baseball leagues, the Tuskegee Airmen, Booker T. Washington, W.E.B. Dubois, Ida B. Wells and Sojourner Truth, Charles Houston and his student—Thurgood Marshall, David Walker, Nat Turner and Harriet Tubman had always been honored in the community, but now, the spirits of Shaka Zulu, Queen Nzinga, Imhotep, and Queen of Sheba had re-evolved.
>
> (p. 152)

Mama C used her novel as an opportunity to introduce readers to the roll call of people she read and learned about beyond the school walls. Ultimately she wanted readers—especially young readers growing up in decaying housing project throughout Brooklyn, to know that there were possibilities awaiting them. Many of the Banneker teachers chose to add *Maurya's Seed* to their English Language Arts curriculum and students were thrilled to have the living and breathing author working in the building. Mama C's hope was that students would learn, much like Passion, that they were the descendents of men and women who were actively engaged in seeking freedom, education, humane housing and lives for their families:

> I've always called [my students] heroes nobody has heard of and I make them write about themselves all the time in the future tense and what has yet to come. I believe that if they envision [their future] then there is a better chance of that happening because our kids need more of that than they need of anything else. There's nothing wrong with them intellectually. They just have so many other problems to deal with and they've been beaten down on so many different levels that they're not even considering the importance of education . . . It's like if you've

been beaten all your life you are not sure if you want education. You're not sure you even want to live.

(interview, March 10, 2004)

Like Brooks's pedagogy of possibility, Mama C saw the primary scope of her work with young people as helping them "envision" their future. Her methodology was a combination of Brooks's role in her workshops as a "friend" in writing, *Black News*'s relentless confrontation of mis-education, and the inter- and cross-generational relationships in Black bookstore and open mic events. Mama C used literacy to breathe life into her students' dreams. Among those "heroes nobody has heard of" was Naja. Naja was a bright-eyed senior who insisted on coming to class even after she graduated mid-semester. Although she grew up in Brooklyn, she had roots in Savannah, Georgia as well as Barbados, West Indies. Naja had worked with Mama C throughout her tenure at Banneker and was always writing and filling up journals (which she always labeled "poetry in progress"). Naja also filled our inboxes with poetry that she wrote between sessions. When Naja came to one of the first classes in a Black Panther t-shirt with the quote, "The struggle continues" across the top she had no idea she was setting the tone for class.

"You Should Be On fire": Developing A Spoken Word Curriculum

The "Spoken Wordologists" were a community of student artists who volunteered to stay after school two days a week to read their poetry aloud or "cipher" with their peers and teachers. This was not an official class—that is, students did not receive credit towards graduation for their participation. Although the group operated like a rotating collective, there were five core members who came to class without fail. Mama C wanted to maintain an open door policy because she believed different students needed the group at different points in their lives; therefore no student was made to feel guilty if they missed sessions. Student poets brought their journals, notebooks, scraps of paper and jumped up to read much like the Anansi Writers' Workshop in South Central Los Angeles described by Michael Datcher earlier in this book. Students, Mama C, and Sister T used each other's words and energy in the circle and continuously read until everyone was finished. Sometimes students would make requests to their peers and teachers to read poems they shared in previous sessions. After everyone read and heard everything they wanted for the day we would sit and talk about topics and ideas that emerged from the poetry, current issues in the news, and update each other on different community events. The Spoken Wordologists had their own Black Study Circle; everyone was invited to participate whether they had new work or not. When students did not have a new piece, they were asked to share old work. This program also had elements of POSA discussed in the previous chapter; the group discussed events in the news and updates about stories in various newspapers. Much like the culture of the Black Arts and Black Power Movements, the circle depended on staying informed and current.

Mama C learned that there was a need for such a program when she discovered that some students wrote poetry and kept journals that never found their way into the traditional curriculum. She explained to me, "[Students] wouldn't have their homework but they had some poetry!" Once they learned that she was interested they would bring their work to her and ask for her feedback. Mama C immediately noted that students had language skills but they did not necessarily realize that they were using literary devices:

> I did teach them language skills . . . I basically showed them that they already [knew] how to use the language because they speak it. They just didn't know the label . . . We all use metaphors and I believe that my people are the most creative speakers. We are colorful with the language and we are very artistic speakers. We are creative in our speech and we have always been that way. Even if it was playing the dozens and the sarcasm that we use but [students] hear the word "sarcastic" and they don't even realize that's figurative language. I just point out to them what they already know . . . I would request that they focus on figurative language in different poems. I would say I want to see more alliteration in this poem and in this poem I want to see more metaphors.
>
> (interview, March 10, 2004)

Scholarship in literacy and culture has challenged deficit models of looking at language minority students by asserting that students bring their "funds of knowledge"—that is linguistic practices, lived experiences, and perspectives from families and communities to the classroom (Gonzalez, Moll, & Amanti, 2005). Mama C's approach with her students' writing was not unlike interventions introduced in Lee's research with the Cultural Modeling Project which seeks to help student speakers of African American Vernacular English (AAVE) use their knowledge and skills to learn literary reasoning (Lee, 2007). Mama C also employed similar strategies seen in urban classrooms such as Joe's Power Writing class (Fisher 2005a, 2005b, 2007a); Joe used student writing as an opportunity to introduce a scientific vocabulary for discussion of literary elements as opposed to introducing the elements in isolation. The process of creating original texts gave students the confidence and passion to be invested in their educational process. The circle also fostered the discourse of literary interpretation.

Using the image of "fire" to encourage students to write, Mama C urged students to read newspapers and stay current. The image of fire has been used in Black cultural production and especially American literature such as James Baldwin's *The Fire Next Time* (1963), and one of the core texts of the Black Arts Movement *Black Fire: an Anthology of Afro American Writing* (1968) edited by LeRoi Jones and Larry Neal. In her study trading the "spirit work" across African American literary traditions, Smith asserts the image of fire "has come to signify the spirited and righteously angry emergence of new generations speaking in new idioms but accountable to the past" (2006, p. 353). Mama C came of age in the "fire" of Ocean Hill-Brownsville when parents fought to have a voice in their children's educational experiences. Now it was time for Mama C's students to name and confront their own fire:

> Consider all the cases in your lifetime, negativity about Black people . . . maybe you believed it. Use writing as revenge. We write from our hearts. Passion guides our writing. I don't want you to walk around angry . . . Don't hate people. Hate racism!
> (Mama C to students, October 14th, 2003)

Mama C modeled using writing as a tool for action. She recently attended a professional development in which the facilitator used the n-word freely and justified her use of it by arguing her students used it. Mama C wrote an article about this experience that was published in a Brooklyn community newspaper called *Our Times Press* which published a three part interview with Jitu Weusi about Ocean Hill-Brownsville. The students wanted to take the action a step further and began to craft a choreopoem that became a mantra for the group:

A nigger I am not
A nigger I never will be
I am not afraid of freedom
Or prosperity.

After the chant, students read individual poems that focused on racism and used the chorus as an introduction, transition, and closing. The choreopoem became the group's signature piece when they performed for the school or at local events. The "fire" continued in the spring semester when a young man, Timothy Stansbury, was murdered by a New York police officer. By all accounts, Stansbury was using his project rooftop to access the building next door because the front doors of his building were not working. A "startled" police officer shot and killed an unarmed Stansbury on the roof leaving residents—and youth in particular—outraged and feeling powerless. Mama C insisted that her students remember Stansbury's name and write something in his honor that could be published or read at one of the public events:

Mama C: People should be on fire right now. This brotha was killed for being on a rooftop in his own building.

Student: Thank you!

Mama C: The cop walks. The cop still has a job.

Student: What? [The cop] still has a job?

Mama C: You should know this you should know this young man's name.

Student: Yo, that is wrong.

Mama C: Just like you should know Amadou Diallo's [name]. This continues on and on and on and we as Black people have to stop it.

Student: Timothy Stansbury.

Mama C: Yes. Please write his name down right now.

Stansbury's death represented a growing fire that was inside many of the students; they feared their lives were becoming disposable. Indeed the fire image was the impetus for Mama C's young heroes. While this energy resembled concerns raised by *Black News* in the late 1960s and early 1970s, scholars warn against the temptation to view the passion of the iconic fire image as a monolithic embodiment of Black writing. Smith (2006) argues that the image of fire "gathers force and signifies the continuity of the black liberation struggle" and "becomes a thread of living tradition" (p. 354). This lens is useful for examining Mama C's pedagogical practices; students are not only reclaiming—to use Baker's (1988) analysis of black aesthetics in literature—but also inventing new cultural products that explicitly reflect their realities. Mama C's living history informs her students' work but leaves room to address old struggles with new responses.

Language, literature, and history were among the tools used in Mama C's writing community to foster inquiry and new ways of thinking about old ideas or what LeRoi Jones/Amiri Baraka has called "the changing same" (1971). At the beginning of the academic year the Spoken Wordologists voted to read *Assata: An Autobiography* by Assata Shakur. Shakur's autobiography shared her journey as a young woman coming of age in North Carolina and New York and her eventual involvement with Civil Rights and Black Power Movements in poetry and prose. Currently a political exile in Cuba, Shakur's story has been resurrected by Black youth culture and hip hop artists in songs, art, and other struggles for social justice. A few months before I met Mama C and her student poets, *VIBE* magazine published an article about Shakur. When I learned that students were reading *Assata* I brought copies of "The Life of an Outlaw" by poet and author Asha Bandele to class. Bandele noted that 30 years had passed since the incident involving Shakur and New Jersey troopers took place in which Shakur was shot three times. Mama C not only used Shakur's autobiography to historicize current social injustices but also because it detailed Shakur pushing herself to become well read and more knowledgeable in American and World history. By her own accounts, Shakur entered college with little political literacy and became embarrassed about how little she knew about the Vietnam War in comparison to some of her peers. Shakur, whose struggle was documented in *Black News*, goes on to describe her experiences at Manhattan Community College she participated in a Black student organization called "The Golden Drums" who fought for the inclusion of a Black Studies program and also hosted campus events. Among these events were lectures that focused on Black and American History:

> The subject of one of the many lectures scheduled by the Drums was about a slave who had plotted and planned an fought for his freedom. Right here in amerika. Until then my only knowledge of the history of Africans in amerika was about George Washington Carver making experiments with peanuts and

about the Underground Railroad . . . The day i found out about Nat Turner I was affected so strongly it was physical. I was so souped up on adrenaline i could barely contain myself. I tore through every book my mother had. Nowhere could i find the name Nat Turner.

(Shakur, 1987, p. 175)

Shakur, like Mama C, grew up "believing the slaves hadn't fought back" (p. 175). The discovery that there were Blacks who did fight back was so compelling to Shakur and Mama C much like Brooks's newly discovered Black pride that it served as an awakening for them to read more, learn more, and most importantly engage in struggle. And like countless recollections of Black children in the United States, Shakur described the shame she felt when slavery was the topic at school. The omission of historiographies detailing Black self-determination and self reliance rendered younger generations hopeless and helpless. The Black Power and subsequently the Black Arts Movements sought to eradicate the lack of self-knowledge and self-worth. Shakur's mis-education of sorts led her to become an avid reader:

You couldn't catch me without a book in my hand after that. I read everything from J.A. Rogers to Julius Lester. From Sonia Sanchez to Haki Madhubuti (Don L. Lee). I saw plays by Black playwrights like Amiri Baraka and Ed Bullins. It was amazing. A whole new world opened up to me. I was also meeting a lot of sisters and brothers whose level of consciousness was much higher than mine—*Black people who had gained knowledge not only by reading but by participating in the struggle* [my emphasis], who talked about Denmark Vesey, Gabriel Prosser, Cinque, as well as Nat Turner, because they had gone out of their way to learn about our history and our struggle.

(p. 175)

Here Shakur echoes Weusi's argument that literacy and reading in particular was core principles of being activists. Shakur recalled that the men and women she was meeting were reading and acting; reading went hand in hand with struggling. Shakur's story was used to help students understand that people could mindfully educate themselves. Mama C's class was about creating and nurturing the desire to want to know. The first day students got their copies of the text, Mama C asked them to put them away. Mama C put her copy in the hands of one student and asked everyone to take turns reading aloud. Once a reader was finished, he or she passed the book to the next person. This passing felt like an energy surge and students were free to stop reading, comment, discuss aspects of the text during the process. At the end of the first *Assata* reading circle Mama C introduced "The Assata Shakur Project" (see Appendix C) which included analyzing the opening poem in *Assata* entitled "Affirmation," creating a timeline of the events in Shakur's life, writing from the perspective of Shakur, and finally writing a poem to Shakur. Mama C thought the project would last throughout the semester but the Spoken Wordologists devoured the book and began writing feverishly. Naja's poem, "The Greatest Threat," prompted the Spoken Wordologists to reconsider the name of their group:

WHERE ARE MY RUNAWAY SLAVES OF THE 21ST CENTURY?
Chorus: RIGHT HERE
Let me school you on this piece of history
The Greatest Threat
To the threads that sew us into a classless stature
Where being human doesn't matter
Where laying next to 'your brotha' in a body bag
Is on the regular
It's like century old shackles that start to make your skin sag
It's the pounding in your chest
A bullet shot
Or 2 or 3
WHO SHOT YA, ASSATA?
My African queen
Whose jewels have been tarnished and twisted
Yet your feet
God has kissed your feet
You've escaped
The slave masters who have yet to master
The magic of your magnificent departure
RUN BUTTERFLY RUN
Until our pain crusts over and festers
Shout out the fallen ones for they need to salvation comes not
    from a gun

And don't worry I'll read to your grandbabies
I'll read so poetically and profound
I'll read as if you were me
SO PURR ON BLACK CAT
Cuz one day you'll roam back
Into the psyche of those stricken with un-remembrance
And then you and I shall dance
As if the African soil tickles our toes again
We won't be ENSLAVED then
Or RUNAWAY ROYALTY of the 21st Century
We'll be free

In her poem Naja compared Shakur's escape from prison to the efforts of runaway slaves. Referring to the prison guards as "slave masters," Naja documented "the magic" of Shakur's "magnificent departure" in the way a caterpillar is transformed in a cocoon in order to become a butterfly. Naja's poem captured the mystery that still surrounds Shakur's escape from prison—something Shakur never reveals in her autobiography. Although Shakur escaped prison, she does not deny the strain this choice had on her mother, aunt and especially her daughter. Naja assured Shakur that she will read to the grandbabies who will not know their grandmother's voice "as if you were me." This symbolic passing of the fire is also evident in Naja's ending of an either real or imagined reunion between her and Shakur:

And I wrote the piece to [Assata Shakur]. The piece basically it starts off "Where are my runaway slaves of the 21st Century" and that's basically calling for all the revolutionary poets out there. Because in *her* book, *she* said she was a runaway slave of the 20th Century so I said we were the runaway slaves of the 21st Century. Then I just started talking to Assata telling her I understand that you can't come home and I will read to your grandbaby. I think the line was "I will read to your grandbaby as if you were me . . ." I said "God has kissed your feet." I talk about how she escaped prison in the poem and how they still haven't figured out how she could do it. It was the magic of her. Basically that's what my poem is about.

(Naja, April 2004)

As the academic year progressed, Naja continued to keep Shakur's name and spirit in her writing. After reading a collection of poetry by a local poet Gerren Liles, Naja made connections between Liles's poem and her prior knowledge of Shakur's autobiography:

> The enslaved mothers were the ones who emancipated the rest
> They cooked, taught, and cleaned up our mess
> There were so many Rosas, Assatas, or Corettas that it was
>   pointless
> To ever accept the fact we are hoes or bitches, we were God sent

Here, Naja contemplated a shift in values across generations. In spite of the different responses to racial injustice within the Black Panther Party and the non-violence sector in the Civil Rights Movement, Naja situated Shakur with the "Rosas" (Rosa Parks) and the "Corettas" (Coretta Scott King). In fact, Shakur notes in her autobiography the growing tensions in her New York chapter of the Black Panther Party as she voiced some of her concerns about the methods towards liberation. Finally, Naja critiques misogyny and disregard for women that she believed were becoming too common in the music of her generation. Naja and Mama C also used history to negotiate their relationship with youth cultural productions.

Reclaiming History: Hip hop, Spoken Word, and Youth Culture

Mama C firmly believed that hip hop music and culture brought back the practice of "listening for the line" for youth. For this reason, Mama C saw a particular value in students' appreciation for this genre in music. Brooklyn hip hop artists like Dead Prez, Mos Def, and Talib Kweli set a tone for what has been referred to as conscious hip hop music. Mama C wanted to build on the culture of listening she considered to be a powerful part of the genre:

> I have always done some spoken word or poetry and used it as inspiration or a topic [for writing]. I've always had students doing literary critiques . . . and I guess just over the years the more that rap grew as a major part of our culture it just dawned on me that the kids are listening more or better than they used to. They are a little more in tune to what's spoken, period. If I

[performed] a poem for them I'd have them. Students can all be quiet but they are not listening ... but if I was doing spoken word, if I would recite for them they were right there. They were on it.

(interview, March 10, 2004)

Mama C argued that hip hop prepared many students to become active listeners. Because spoken word poetry honored rhythm, cadence, and storytelling, students were invested in using it as a tool for engaging other literate practices. Many hip hop artists have confronted mis-education in their lyrics. To be sure, Brooklyn-based Dead Prez critiqued representations of Black Americans in the curriculum in their song "They schools": "I tried to pay attention but they classes wasn't inter-estin'. They seemed to only glorify the Europeans/Claiming Africans were only three-fifths a human being." (2000). Purposefully using African American Vernacular English ("they schools" and "they classes"), Dead Prez demonstrate their unwillingness to accept ideologically biased knowledge. The group, made up of M-1 and stic.man, situate themselves as being on the periphery of a pubic school system they believed had little, if any, interest in them as young, African American males. Their testimony further supports both Mama C and Shakur's missed opportunities as young learners to understand slavery through multiple perspectives; the master narrative in schools omitted the David Walkers, Nat Turners, Denmark Veseys, and Sojourner Truths. Another Brooklyn-based group Black Star (Mos Def and Talib Kweli), urged urban youth to uncover the privilege of "K.O.S." or "Knowledge of Self-Determination." Black Star, named after Marcus Garvey's famous Black Star Line of ships intended to transport Black people from the United States and the Caribbean to the continent of Africa, did not focus their critique on schools. In the context of "K.O.S" education was a personal journey: "That's why, Knowledge of Self is like life after death/Apply it, to your life, let destiny manifest" (1999). The tensions in hip hop culture were also addressed in Mama C's class and she made her position transparent to students in the beginning of the spring semester when new students joined the circle:

I have nothing against hip hop. I love all art forms. I don't love vulgarity. If you're cursing to the beat that's not useful for me. You know what I'm saying? I'd rather give you some history, some truth, okay? Some righteousness and conditions that are going on right now.

Mama C held class at Nkiru Books—a landmark Black bookstore in Brooklyn that Mos Def and Talib Kweli purchased in order to keep it open when the owner experienced financial difficulties. Mama C believed it was the perfect location to host Abiodun Oyewole, a member of the The Last Poets, who participated in the "poets in the schools" program. In this particular session, Oyewole underscored what he conceptualized as a continuum between student work and the history of language for African Americans:

> We have been living in a world of bastardization of words for some time where we are not really getting the sacredness out of the words we deserve—that we need. And poetry is the only sacred language we've got left. But the fact is we have a lot of folks who need to express themselves and poetry is still that language that allows us to tell the truth and at the same time give it some flavor and some spice.
>
> (2003)

Known for their uncensored testimonials to Black life during the 1960s and 1970s in inner city neighborhoods throughout the United States, The Last Poets are often hailed as the forefathers of hip hop. Oyewole's service to New York City public schools was consistent with Mama C's youth advocacy. Naming poetry as the vehicle for preserving the "sacredness" of words, Oyewole acknowledged the "need" for such expression throughout the history of Africans in the Americas. Referring to poetry as a language, Oyewole further noted the power in telling the "truth" with "flavor" and "spice." Oyewole's characterization of the "bastardization of words" was a reference to the strategic of African language patterns in an effort to minimize communication among and between enslaved Africans. Students like Naja understood Oyewole's poetry and Mama C's after school movement to be a history course as well as a writing seminar:

> You have spoken word and spoken word is a tool to relate a message. And it's not just when you go to history class and someone gives a lecture on history. Most people feel threatened

by a lecture but spoken word is an art. You can give them a message and so much meaning.

(Naja, April 20, 2004)

Naja considered spoken word as a methodology for teaching and learning history; however, she contrasted the style and delivery of spoken word to a history class lecture. According to Naja, a lecture could be threatening "to most people" whereas spoken word could "relate a message" through art. Embedded in Naja's feedback is her belief that art makes learning more accessible. Naja's statement also critiques the "banking model" concept of education where the teacher "deposits" information into students (Freire, 2003) and supports methods used by Brooks, the Black Study Circle described in *Black News*, and the inter-generational out-of-school literacy communites:

> Spoken word is history itself. Like it started, [Mama C] started teaching us the tradition of griots and it starts with the word of mouth. All history started with the word of mouth. Every story that was told, every fable, every myth started with the word of mouth. That's what spoken word is. We're just continuing that tradition. It's evolved and it's growing into a whole industry now but its origins are in history. It's used to tell history, to preserve history. That's why it's such a powerful tool because it is history.
>
> (Naja, April 20, 2004)

In his study of griots and griottes, Hale (1998) contends that the "texts" of griots "provide deep insights into the values of a people and their social structure" (p. 23). Hale also argues that contributions from griots to African history cannot be minimized solely because they are "oral rather than written" (p. 24). Much like the "great divide" debates that influenced early scholarship in literacy research, Hale's study of griots further complicates the notion of a hierarchy in these forms of communication. Naja considered her poetry and the writing of her peers as "continuing that tradition" while acknowledging an increased popu-larity of spoken word in television programming and anthologies (Fisher, 2004; Smith, 2006). Naja ultimately linked the medium of spoken word to oral histories while demonstrating an understanding of the role of griots in West Africa as well as the power of orality. Scholars have examined African American extensions of the griot:

African American poets extend the griot, or bardic, tradition by performing their poetry in formal and informal reading and recitations before audiences. The silent reader, too, becomes an active participant in the language situation as she or he hears with the inner ear and praises (or dismisses) the written text.

(Brown, 1999, p. 26)

Mama C attempted to make meaningful connections with African and African American history. The spoken word poetry curriculum addressed the discovery of the remains of enslaved Africans, widely known as the African Burial Ground, near Wall Street in Manhattan. The African Burial Ground project, in conjunction with the Schomburg Center for Research in Black Culture,[2] provided materials for educators including timelines, maps and a wealth of information about the excavation. Some of the sessions were devoted to research on the African Burial Ground. One day the discussion inevitably blended into a discussion of the recent school trip to Senegal and Ghana, West Africa which Mama C and Naja attended. Because Naja went on this trip with a particular awareness following the reading and discussions of slavery in New York City, she was disappointed in her peers who showed more interest in shopping rather than visiting the preserved holding caves for enslaved Africans being sent to the Americas. Naja expressed this disappointment through her poem "Shopping Spree":

Money flashing, lies and deceptions
The Miseducation of these Negroes
Who rather sing Lauryn Hill on buses
Instead of visiting slave castles
And questioning why their titles are not dungeons
And in 50 years I fear
My experience of Senegal will be
In the lost and dumbfounded

Signifying on Carter G. Woodson's classic text *The Mis-education of the Negro* and rapper/singer Lauryn Hill's album "The Miseducation of Lauryn Hill," Naja questioned her peers' lack of interest visiting the "slave castles" in Senegal. Naja was even more "dumbfounded" by her peers' inability to question why "slave castles" were not called "dungeons." Mama C encouraged Naja to read her poem at a school event to begin a school wide discussion about the trip. In the closing of her poem, Naja hypothetically asks a Senegalese craftsmen "How much for a piece of dignity?" This final question demonstrated Naja's exasperation with the trip becoming a "shopping spree" for most of the participants. Naja, in a very sophisticated manner, confronted complicated issues about capitalism and the enduring exploitation of African countries. Naja's courage and insight to confront the issues grew out of the support she received in the spoken word class. It was in the poetry circle that Naja asked for feedback and generated strategies to prepare students for future travel/study programs.

Toward a Literocracy: Building the Next Movement

Naja asserted that she saw her participation in the spoken word poetry class as an opportunity to work on her writing skills across genres and content areas in addition to a course in history. Poetry helped Naja gain writing confidence; she began to approach her writing from the perspective that if she could get comfortable with language and using words to work for her, than writing would be more enjoyable:

> For me, personally, I love writing all different kinds of writing. I don't shy away from having to write an essay but essays are boring sometimes. So with the use of poetry, and you know poetry doesn't have to rhyme, so you can have poetry in your essays and you can manipulate words that other people can't do because they don't get the opportunity to play with words like I do . . . *The most important tool is knowing the English language and knowing how to use it because people who know how to use the English language won't get confused by it* [emphasis added]— won't get trapped by it.
>
> (interview, April, 20, 2004)

Naja identified the trappings of being unfamiliar and uncomfortable with language. Through writing poetry, Naja began to "manipulate words." Naja's "play" with words which gave her a sense of ownership and extinguished any fear associated with writing. In an early phase in her academic career, Naja was already ascribing a sense of power to language as well as the sense of "sacredness" projected by Oyewole's visit to Mama C's class. Naja also believed being a poet helped her in an oratorical competition; once again acknowledging the links between spoken word poetry and history:

> I might say something in my essay that sounds poetic and people will say "That's so poetic. You can tell you're a poet." *Because I play with words and I switch around sounds and you don't have to start an essay off with "My essay is about" or "My thesis statement is." You use the language, use the words that you're taught in school* [emphasis added]. I remember I had to do an oratorical competition and the last sentence we had to talk about a figure so I talked about Harriet Tubman and I said "Just as Harriet Tubman once did, I will venture out into the wilderness and face every obstacle and I will reach back to pull my generation to that Promised Land." And everybody said "That's so poetic." But it wasn't even a poem it was an essay. When you learn how to use words like how you want them and to enjoy words, you'll have an easier time writing essays.
>
> (interview, April 20, 2004)

Naja considered writing poetry an opportunity to use words "how you want them" with the ability to "switch around sounds" and use different literary devices to convey her message. Even in her discussion of writing, Naja still made explicit links with history using Harriet Tubman's life as a metaphor for her work with youth. Perhaps most importantly, Naja used her words to inspire and organize her peers. She sought opportunities to share her writing at school events, on local radio programs, and with community institutions who fought against poverty, social injustice, and mis-education. By contextualizing Mama C's classroom in King's concept of "Critical Studyin'" visible in IBIs, I attempted to demonstrate the inter- and cross-generational work of Mama C and Naja. In the process of "Critical Studyin'," Mama C and her students co-created literocracy—that is a democratic space for exploring, analyzing and synthesizing ideas using history, literature, and creativity (Fisher, 2005a, 2005b). Challenging ideologically-biased knowledge, Mama C's after school class was both an "alternative" and "supplementary" learning space with values rooted in Freedom School traditions (Fisher, 2006a). The Spoken Wordologists, or The Runaway Slaves of the 21st Century, reclaimed the ingenuity of enslaved Africans who founded "secret schools" (Holt, 1990), African American readers and writers in the early nineteenth century who created literary societies (McHenry & Heath, 1994; McHenry, 2002), organizers of Citizenship Schools and Freedom Schools (King, 2006), educators who founded and maintained IBIs such as newspapers, schools, and community centers, and the "fire" of the Black Arts and Black Power Movements (Lee, 1992; Fisher, 2004). Mama C did what countless parents did in the late 1960s and early 1970s; she re-defined "within a community context the possibilities and gifts that Black children offer the world" (Lee, 1992, p. 161). To be sure, Naja applied her writing and speaking skills in other areas of her education by using writing to think critically about her community and eventually the world. Towards the end of the academic year a very calm and peaceful looking Mama C addressed her students in the circle:

> You are the hope. You are definitely the hope because you are going to pass it on. You're not going to sit by and just let this stuff go down. I'm not concerned about the future at all. Not at all. Because we have too many children out there who know what the deal is, who know what they have to do, and who are not going to allow the slavery to come back. You're not going to have it. You're not going to let your kids be raised ignorantly. You're not going to have it. So I'm fine. I'm not worried about it at all.
>
> (interview, April 20, 2004)

In an effort to light one last "fire" in her students, Mama C conveyed her confidence and trust in the circle. She attempted to build an institution founded on respect and, to borrow Black Star's term, "Knowledge of Self-Determination" (K.O.S) through reading, writing, orality, and most importantly action. Mama C and her students created a newish voice, in the same way that Brooks developed hers, *Black News* did for their readership and Black youth in particular and in forums like POSA and the Jahva House Speak Easy, that could be carried outside of the school and into the many spaces her students would travel. Together they rediscovered and invented Black cultural products and moved toward a literocracy—that is, an intersection of literate practices and democratic engagement (Fisher, 2005a, 2005b, 2007a). Naja and her peers with the guidance of artist-activist-teachers like Mama C learned that writing served a purpose much larger than the craft itself. For the Spoken Wordologists writing, reading, and speaking were political acts that

challenged ideologically-biased knowledge and acts that had consequences beyond the walls of Banneker and into their communities.

Catching and Keeping the Fire

In her poem "Catch the fire (for Bill Cosby)," poet, activist, and teacher
Sonia Sanchez asks "Where is your fire?" to reimagine what the "fire"
found in the Black Arts and Black Power Movements might look like for
a new generation. Responding to actor, comedian Bill Cosby's concern
that Black youth were losing their "fire" and consequently their
commitment to themselves and each other, Sanchez responded with a
poem urging youth to not only "catch the fire" but most importantly
"pass it on" to others. During a recent visit to Emory University, Sanchez
and colleagues revisited the Black Arts Movement. Sanchez noted that she
and countless poets in the movement were part of "history and herstory"
while "changing the world." While Sanchez discussed many aspects of the
Black Arts Movement, she emphasized the activism and advocacy of a
librarian at the Schomburg, Jean Hutson, who introduced Sanchez to
books written by, for, and about Black people. Ms. Hutson sent a young
Sanchez to the aforementioned Micheaux's bookstore where he had a bag
of books waiting for her that Ms. Hutson requested. Sanchez shared this
story to underscore that the Black Arts Movement was a "generational
movement" in which one did not just keep the information he or she
received but it was their responsibility to "give it to the youth."[3]

Black literate lives demonstrate that reading, writing, and speaking is
always an act of struggle or as Assata Shakur articulated in her
autobiography, "Black people who gained knowledge not only by reading
but also by participating in the struggle" (1987, p. 175). In educational
research and more specifically literacy research, these historiographies
and ethno-histories map a rich, longstanding continuum of activism
around words. This is not to say the crafting of words and language to
be creative, artistic, and at times playful does not have a very important place in Black traditions which certainly scholars like Geneva
Smitherman and Fahamisha Patricia Brown have shown. With that said,
words simply on display could not sustain a people who had to
reconstruct their humanity for themselves and others after being viewed
and treated as chattel and subhuman. In order to understand the
pedagogy of possibility, one must understand that for Black writers,
speakers, teachers, and activists words must work.

Throughout this book education in the context of Black lives is synonymous with literacy. In these lived struggles, literacy is not a means to an end or focused on individual advancement. Literacy was used to move an entire race forward educationally, socially, economically, and politically. The Black Arts and Black Power Movements refueled the "fire" of self-reliance and self-determination. In the turbulent 1960s when these movements took root, Black people found themselves enslaved again in other ways; their values, ideas, and contributions were not represented in the literary canons, mainstream presses or publishing houses and certainly missing in action in public school curriculum. Black people were—and in many ways still are—trying to find a space to both catch and keep the fire as evidenced in the work of PLCs and Mama C's classroom. Brooks discovered one of these spaces when she attended the 1967 Black Writers' Conference and eventually recreated them for young people through anthologies and writing workshops. *Black News* also forged a space through their reporting on public schools, housing and promoting reading and acting. The fire in these contexts, as well as twenty-first century institutions, have focused on moving together and fostering a non-competitive philosophy found in Nyerere's teachings of African socialism. Taking David Walker's lead, these institutions resisted isolating the perceived "illiterate" by seeking to engage from the grandmothers to the militants and from the teachers to the students. In sum, there was no grouping or tracking because how well one did for him or herself was of no consequence if he or she did not return to help others.

Mama C brought the fire she received from the "new Blacks" as a child in Ocean Hill-Brownville and passed it to the Spoken Wordologists. Mama C was not at all unlike a young Weusi when he first found himself teaching in a segregated classroom in a public school system. "What shall I tell my children who are Black?" was not solely a poem Weusi used as a pedagogical tool with his Black students; this poem was simultaneously an indictment and a call that Black children deserved to know their history and be challenged to participate in the struggle. Indeed, Margaret Burrough's poem is as relevant in today's current educational climate of educational inequities and poverty as it was when Weusi used it in his classroom. Black children—and all children—must participate in the living tradition of Black history that Marable argues (2006). In an ambitious volume that re-reads and reinterprets the Black Arts Movement, Smith asserts:

The rediscovery and invention of cross-generational ties are a strategic construction serving specific literary, cultural, and political needs at the turn of the twenty-first century, rather than a natural inheritance of essential and immanent blackness, as it is often represented. This constructedness in no way diminishes the intensity of the "fire" of tradition or its social and political efficacy. A bridge that has been repaired may, in fact, be stronger than the original.

(Smith, 2006, p. 356)

The Black Arts and Black Power Movements repositioned Black poets, writers and activists as powerful and worthy while redefining who got counted as literate and knowledgeable as well as what got counted as literacy and knowledge. Mama C returned agency and powerful literacies to her students which made them want to learn and, most importantly, desire to live. Black literate lives are so much more than the so-called great divide in literacy research. It is time for educators to ask what they will tell the children—all of whom will benefit from revisiting these histories and become a part of the current struggle.

Acknowledgments

Parts of this chapter appear in "Building a Literocracy: Diaspora Literacy and Heritage Knowledge in Participatory Literacy Communities" in A. Ball's (Ed.) *With more deliberate speed: Achieving equity and excellence in education—Realizing the full potential of Brown v. Board of Education* and is reprinted with permission from the National Society for the Study of Education.

Notes on Methodology

This study employs both "ethnohistory" (Heath, 1981) and "historical ethnography" (Siddle-Walker, 1996) methods. Heath argues that ethnohistories are needed to understand the context in which various communities use writing. Historical ethnography mirrors ethnohistory in that it is a method deeply committed to context; however, it is not solely focused on examining writing.

In Chapters 1 and 2 I re-read historiographies of the Black struggle for education and thus literacy using the lens of a literacy researcher. As a graduate student I became keenly interested in historical perspectives of how Black people in the context of the United States engaged in acts of reading, writing, speaking, and "doing." Few studies existed in educational research that examined the relationships and fluidity of these entities. Literacy research, in particular, largely focused on an oral and literate dichotomy or what has been referred to as the great divide. I had to piece together research from education, history, and cultural studies to construct an understanding of the literacy practices of Black people. I yearned for a source that synthesized this research and made it accessible for an education research community. Elizabeth McHenry and Shirley Brice Heath (1994) began this work in their study "The literate and the literary: African Americans as writers and readers 1830–1940." A decade later I attempted to begin where McHenry and Heath finished in "The

song is unfinished: The new literate and literary and their institutions"
(2004) by examining post-Harlem Renaissance literary movements and
communities. My point of departure from McHenry and Heath's major
contributions to the field was not only the time period but also social
class. McHenry and Heath argued that the contribution of middle-class
and upper middle-class blacks to the literary arts are often undermined.
My research, however, focuses on the Black Power and Black Arts
Movements that were vehemently opposed class distinctions among
Blacks and who consequently believed poetry and writing belonged to
the people.

In Chapter 3, I employed archival research methods and document
analysis to analyze a collection of *Black News* newspapers out of the EAST
organization in Brooklyn, New York. My father, James A. Fisher, gave me
a set of the newspapers. Each issue had been preserved in sheet protectors
and my father, a historian by trade, even included correspondence with
Black News about some confusion with his subscription. Additionally I
consulted mailings sent out by *Black News* and the EAST organization to
the newspaper subscribers and supporters. So why use *Black News* when
there is a wealth of historic black periodicals? *Black News* was especially
compelling because it was founded in the wake of the Ocean Hill-
Brownsville crisis and was therefore critically invested in issues of public
school education as they related to Black people in the United States and
abroad. In addition to reading every newspaper and keeping analytic
notes, I looked for patterns and themes in each issue. All articles written
about educational opportunities offered through the EAST organization
and the community were of particular interest and I paid close attention
to articles that gave me some idea about what pedagogies were valued in
the context of *Black News* as well as the philosophical underpinnings of
such values. When the newspaper staff cited articles, literature, and other
historical documents, I searched for the primary sources. I also looked
at other documents produced during the tenure of *Black News* that
discussed Independent Black Institutions (IBIs) such as the Council of
Independent Black Institutions (CIBI) documents, conference and
workshop papers on community control, pamphlets, and periodicals.

And while I sought to contextualize the history of the newspaper
through the collection itself and supporting documents created during
the newspaper's tenure, I was missing the human voice of the newspaper.
At the time I was conducting this research the only comprehensive study
I could find that discussed *Black News* newspaper and the EAST, was

Kwasi Konadu's (2005) *Truth crushed to the earth shall rise again: The EAST organization and the principle and practices of Black nationalist development*. It was through e-mail exchanges with Professor Konadu that I was able to obtain the contact information for Jitu Weusi (formerly known as Les Campbell and "Big Black") who was one of the newspaper's founders and the headmaster of Uhuru Sasa Shule. Mr. Weusi— or Baba Weusi as I call him—was gracious enough to grant me an interview which was open-ended and conducted much like an oral history. The interview took place on Wednesday, March 21, 2007 at the Schomburg Center for Research in Black Culture in Harlem and Sisters Caribbean Cuisine also in Harlem. I wish to note that as we walked from the Schomburg on 135th Street and Lenox Avenue/Malcolm X Boulevard to Sisters Caribbean Cuisine on 124th many people recognized and stopped Baba Weusi. The first, a young African American man, yelled "Professor! Professor!" as we were crossing the street (and no, he was not talking to me). This young man invited Baba Weusi to an organizing meeting to help a long-term African American record store owner in Harlem fight an unexpected eviction. Next we were stopped by an older African American man who was sitting outside of his building marveling over the gentrification taking place on his block. Last we were stopped by two other older African American men on 125th Street who expressed awe at seeing Baba Weusi and repeatedly told him how good it was to still see him living. This, of course, was an implicit acknowledgement that many of Weusi's peers and organizers of *Black News* and the EAST had passed away.

After the first interview, Baba Weusi granted a second interview on his turf in Brooklyn, New York. The second interview took place on Tuesday, April 24, 2007 at A&B Bookstore, Dare Bookstore (both Black-owned and operated bookstores) and a neighborhood eatery called Night of the Cookers. For the second interview we focused questions about the newspaper and its focus on education and its role in establishing Uhuru Sasa Shule. It is important to note that Baba Weusi's openness is extraordinary considering that he experienced the infiltration of the United States government in Black organizations through COINTELPRO that severed relationships and planted the seeds of distrust, thus strategically dividing and conquering Black activists. In fact, members of the *Black News* staff later learned that one of their fellow colleagues was a government agent and largely responsible for the loss of a grant they applied for in order to purchase their own printing press.

Chapters 4 and 5 include data from two ethnographies I conducted. In Chapter 4, I revisit data from my dissertation research on what I refer to as Participatory Literacy Communities (PLCs). From 2002–2003 I was a participant observer at two Black-owned and operated bookstore events and two spoken word poetry open mic events in Northern California. In addition to being a participant observer, I interviewed some 70 participants ranging in ages 16–60 who were event organizers, poets, featured authors, and members of the audience. All interviews were transcribed by my grandmother, Arlis Fisk, who worked as a transcriber for the State of California. All transcribed interviews were coded and examined in relationship to interviews conducted at the same sites as well as across sites. Chapter 4 is a "remix", if you will, of studies published in *Anthropology and Education Quarterly*, *Research in the Teaching of English*, and *Written Communication*.

Chapter 5 draws from data I collected during my postdoctoral research fellowship at Teachers College, Columbia University, during the 2003–2004 academic year. During that year I conducted extended day writing programs in two urban high schools. One program was the Power Writing Seminar in the Bronx, New York (Fisher 2005a, 2005b, 2007a). The second extended day program was the Spoken Wordologists in Brooklyn, New York. Initially I wanted to understand the ways in which English Language Arts teachers in urban high schools used pedagogical tools found in out-of-school settings much like the PLCs I studied in Northern California. When I conceptualized the study, I thought I would include both sites. However, once I became a participant observer in both classes I saw that these were two very different communities. Both focused on youth cultural productions in the medium of spoken word poetry and performance; however, Mama C's Spoken Wordologists were greatly influenced by Mama C's experiences coming of age in Ocean Hill-Brownsville during the struggle for community control. Prior to beginning the study I did not know Mama C grew up in Ocean Hill-Brownsville nor did I know she experienced Uhuru Sasa Shule programming as described in *Black News*. However, it was evident that in order to understand Mama C's poetry circle, I had to understand the history of Ocean Hill-Brownsville before and after the confrontation between Black parents and the United Federation of Teachers in New York City. In addition to being a participant observer and eventually a contributing poet to Mama C's circle, I interviewed Mama C and her core students—that is, students who attended each session relatively without fail. Mama C's interview was conducted in two parts; the first, conducted on February 20, 2004 at Teachers College, Columbia University, employed oral history methodology and the second, conducted at Benjamin Banneker Academy for Community Development on March 10, 2004, focused on specific questions about her work with Black youth in the poetry circle. Naja, the focal student in Chapter 5, was interviewed in the spring of 2004 which was the end of her senior year. I interviewed Naja again in spring 2005 at the end of her first year of college. Since I met Naja in the fall of 2003, we have been in consistent contact via e-mail and telephone. Over the past four years I have collected all of Naja's poems, essays, and other forms of writing.

"The 15 Demands of the African American Students' Association" as printed in *Black News* on December 1, 1969, Volume 1, Number 5, p. 6

1. No more automatic suspension of H.S. Students
2. No more police or police aides inside NYC schools
3. Strict adherence to fire regulations . . . doors to schools must be left open
4. Open the schools daily to parent observation
5. Community rehabilitation centers must be allowed to set up programs to treat known drug addicts in the school buildings
6. Elimination of all General Course of Study
7. Elimination of all Regents Exams
8. Recognition by all NYC schools of two Black Holidays . . . May 19th Malcolm X's birthday . . . January 15th Martin Luther King, Jr.'s birthday
9. Immediate alternation of teaching population and examinations to supply Black educators proportionate to the student population
10. Complete examination of all books and educational supplies and materials used by the schools to their adequacy and relevancy
11. The creation of school clubs along ethnic lines with facilities and funds from the G.O.
12. Improved conditions for the students in the schools, such as music in the lunch rooms, more dances, improved athletic programs with rifle clubs and self defense classes

13. Teachers who are teaching a course have a background related to the course
14. Creation of Student/Faculty Council (equal representation), in each school which will make decisions on the following matters: curriculum, school staff, discipline, rules and regulations, etc.
15. THE REORGANIZATION OF THE HIGH SCHOOLS ALONG COMMUNITY LINES SO THAT BLACK STUDENTS WILL NOT BE FORCED TO GO TO SCHOOLS IN HOSTILE COMMUNITIES TO SEEK AN EDUCATION (FRANKLIN K. LANE, JOHN ADAMS, CANARSIE, ETC . . .)

We are sure that you the Black Community will recognize the long overdue changes that these demands call for. We grew tired of waiting for you adults to really wake up and understand what we have been trying to tell you all these years. Those "so-called" schools you were rushing us off to every morning represented to us cruel prisons where we were sentenced to serve our time without a hope of parole or time off for good behavior until we reached the age of 17. And so dear parents we urge you to join us, but come what may we aren't quitting until we get this job done.

The Assata Shakur Project for Spoken Word/Multicultural Literature

Ms. Wright-Lewis

1. Analyze the first poem in *Assata* entitled, "Affirmation."
   - Discuss and quote at least three different uses of figurative language she uses and rewrite it in your own words
   - Interpret the quotes
   - Explain the theme of the poem
   - Explain the title—what is her affirmation?
2. Create a timeline highlighting the most memorable and horrific events [Shakur] encountered during her life from the time she was born until now:
   - You may need to find additional information about her besides the book. There have been several documentaries done about her on "Like It Is" (Gil Noble's television show).
   - Utilize information from the internet as well.
3. Beginning today pretend you are Assata and create a journal using poetry and/or prose. Describe the events that happen to you from the day you're shot and apprehended until the day you escape:
   - You may use the poetry in the book and answer it or translate it into your own words;
   - You could also focus on other people you encounter and speak through them in your journal;

- You could also react to the different settings you have been forced to live in;
- You can discuss a personality you were introduced to and impressed by through the experience or from being a Black Panther and a member of the Black Liberation Army;
- Remember you are Assata and that only you know how you escaped—tell us how you did it;

Last, but not least, write a poem to Assata—pour your heart out—give her a tribute or just write about the experience.

Due on December 17th.

Notes

An Introduction: Not Yet Free

1 For a comprehensive discussion of Maulana Karenga and the emergence of Kwanzaa see Scot Brown's (2003) *Fighting for US: Maulana Karenga, the US organization, and Black cultural nationalism.*

2 According to the Black United Fund of Sacramento Valley Inc., the original Kwanzaa committee was comprised of Shule Jumamose's founders: the late Cheryl Fisher, Bertha Gaffney Gorman, Martha Tate-Reid, Leroy Willis, Byron Robertson, and Stan St. Amant. The Kwanzaa committee later included: Ramona Armistead, the late Leslie Campbell, Lujuan, Tchaka Muhammad, and Aisha Yetunde.

1 Toward a Theory of Black Literate Lives

1 Robert C. Morris (1981) offers a comprehensive treatment of the Freedmen's Bureau and its role in the education of Blacks in *Reading, 'riting, and reconstruction: The education of freedmen in the South 1861–1870.*

2 See Valerie Kinloch's (2006) *June Jordan: Her life and letters* for a discussion of Jordan's family history and Garveyism as well as its impact on her Poetry for the People program at the University of California, Berkeley.

2 "I Don't Want Us to Forget the Fire"

1 "Bronzeville" was a name bestowed upon the South Side of Chicago denoting it was a largely Black community.

2 In *Report from part one*, Brooks included a section that was written by her mother in Brooks's voice. The story about relieving a young Brooks from housework in order to focus on writing was part of the story her mother shared.

3 Brooks listed her fellow members in the South Side Community Art Center writing workshop in an interview in *Black Books Bulletin* in June 1974 and also in her autobiography *Report from part one* (1972).

4 This conference has been referred to as the "Black Writers Conference" as well as the "Fisk Writers Conference" in various writings.

5 See Mullen's (1999) "Engendering the Cultural Front: Gwendolyn Brooks, Black Women, and Class Struggle in Poetry" in B.V. Mullen's *Popular fronts: Chicago and African-American cultural politics, 1935–1946* for a more comprehensive discussion of the Great Migration.

6 In "The Trumpet of Conscience," King argues that nonviolent techniques could be embraced by people who have been engaged in violent acts "if they can act constructively and express through an effective channel their very legitimate anger" (King, in Washington, 1986, p. 659). Here he recounts his experiences marching with members of the Blackstone Rangers.

7 In Haki Madhubuti's (1973) *From plan to planet*, he provides a reading list for Black people which he called "Toward a functional reading list." Some of the sections included "Afrika/Afrikanism/Colonialism," "Religions and Philosophy," and "Psychology, Sociology, Education and Politics."

8 In a 1973 interview with Hoyt Fuller, Eugenia Collier, George Kent, and Dudley Randall, Brooks talked about starting her reading and writing group with neighborhood children. In an addendum to that interview, Brooks clarified that she was not able to "corral" 30 students but was able to work with 18 students over the course of four years.

9 My emphasis.

3 Agitating, Educating, and Organizing

1 Preston Wilcox (1968) defined community control as "the power to make and enforce the following decisions: a) Expenditure of funds; b) Hiring and firing of all staff; c) Site election and naming of schools; d) Design and construction of schools; e) Purchasing power; f) Setting up of educational policy and programs; and g) Merit pay to staff."

2 See Jerald E. Podair's (2002) *The Strike that changed New York: Blacks, whites, and the Ocean Hill-Brownsville crisis* and Jane A. Gordon's (2001) *Why they couldn't wait: A critique of the Black-Jewish conflict over community control in Ocean Hill-Brownsville, 1967–1971.*

3 These figures were reported by *Black News* co-founder Jitu Weusi during an interview with the author on March 21, 2007, in Harlem, New York. The same figures appear in Konadu's (2005) *Truth crushed to the Earth shall rise again: The EAST organization and the principles and practice of black nationalist development.* New Jersey: Africa World Press. In its June 12, 1970 issue, *Black News* reported the staff printed 15,000 copies of each issue that typically sold out in four days. According to Jitu Weusi, *Black News* had approximately 400 regular subscribers that included the United States, parts of Africa, and the Caribbean.

4 During the 1960s and 1970s, it was common for African Americans to replace birth names also known as "slave names" with Kiswahili names and words. Les Campbell was also known as "Big Black" and later Jitu Weusi. "Jitu" is a Kiswahili word translated as "giant" or "big," and "Weusi" is a Kiswahili word meaning "Black."

5 The *Black News* Staff included Jim Williams, Jim Dyson, Antoinette Brown, Addie Rimmer, Maurice Fredericks, and Don Blackman.

6 The first issue of *Black News* that included *Fundisha* featured Malauna Karenga, founder of the US organization and creator of Kwanzaa on the cover. *Fundisha's* lead article was written by Don L. Lee who was the executive director of the Institute for Positive Education. *Fundisha's* last appearance in *Black News* was April 1974, Volume 2, Number 16 after the EAST withdrew its membership from CAP.

7 When I visited the Apartheid Museum in Johannesburg, South Africa in 2005, the museum dedicated a significant amount of space to the Jim Crow South in the United States, drawing comparisons between segregation and apartheid.

8 Jitu Weusi noted that *Rebellion News* was established in the Roxbury section of Boston, Massachusetts.

9 Al Vann is currently a New York City Council member.

10 In the February 2, 1969 issue of *The Black Panther*, the "10 Point Program and Platform of the Black Student Unions" is published on p. 22.

11 The article was "dedicated to: Adeyemi, Maliki, Shango, Jumibia, Abenn Halden, Doud, Yusef, Monifa, Sia, Karriema, Ife, Nilaja, Kisha, Titanga, Addie, Shieba and all of the many young brothers and sisters who have helped build A.S.A." (*Black News*, December 10, 1970, p. 2)

12 See "The Prelude to the Ocean Hill Brownville Community/Union Confrontation," in *Our Times Press*, December 1, 2006, Volume 11, Number 23 which is Part Two of a three-part series on Jitu Weusi (Les Campbell).

13 For a thorough history of Black cultural nationalist ideologies as introduced by Malauna Karenga's US organization, see Scot Brown's (2003) *Fighting for US: Malauna Karenga, the US organization, and Black cultural nationalism*. New York and London: New York University Press.

14 African leaders and scholars like Kwame Nkrumah of Ghana and Leopold Senghor were held in the same regard. I focus on Nyerere here because Weusi named him as his foremost influence.

15 Wayne Grice was listed as the director for this particular production of Césaire's "A Season in the Congo" and Ralph Manheim was noted as the translator. The advertisement also noted that the production would be held at Long Island University in Brooklyn.

16 According to the advertisement The Harlem School of The Arts' production of "A Season in the Congo" was to be held in JHS 271 auditorium on March 17, 1970.

17 Weusi cited Philip S. Foner's (1950) *The life and writings of Frederick Douglass*, Volume II as his source for "What is your Fourth of July to Me?"

18 The Council of Independent Black Institutions (CIBI) serves as an umbrella organization for African-centered and independent black schools throughout the United States. Founded in 1972, CIBI organizes professional development workshops for teachers and administrators, hosts conferences, and has a speakers bureau. Jitu Weusi was one of many speakers endorsed by CIBI.

4 "The Song Is Unfinished"

1 See L. Muller and the Blueprint Collective's (1995) *Poetry for the people: A revolutionary Blueprint* for a more extensive description of the program including course outlines, sample poetry, and the history of June Jordan's visionary program.

2 "Amara Rashad" is a pseudonym.

3 Eddie Jefferson was a jazz vocalist who wrote lyrics for many instrumental jazz compositions.

4 Dorsey's Locker, a bar and soul food eatery, hosted a spoken word poetry open mic every Tuesday in North Oakland. The owner of the Jahva House Café, D'Wayne Wiggins and the Speak Easy organizer and host Greg Bridges used the open mic at Dorsey's Locker as a blueprint, according to Bridges.

5 Italics = song, roman = poem.

6 These are excerpts from NerCity and Scorpio Blues's poems. It is also important to note that both poets memorized these pieces and the versions here are transcribed from video footage; other versions of these pieces may exist.

7 Some of the published authors who participated in the Anansi Writers' Workshop include Jenoyne Adams, Sequoia Olivia Mercier, and Derrick I. M. Gilbert

8 I attended Datcher's readings for *Raising Fences* at Marcus Books and Carol's Books in 2002.

9 *Nommo* is a West African concept that refers to the "sacred word." See Janheinz Jahn's (1961) *Muntu: African culture and the western world.*

10 Prior to interviewing Gabrilla, I visited the *NOMMO* Literary Society in New Orleans, Louisiana, in April 2002, I interviewed its founder, Kalamu ya Salaam as part of my research on Participatory Literacy Communities. Mr. Salaam was very helpful in recommending books as well as venues to experience readings and performances. My interview with Salaam was conducted prior to Hurricane Katrina; since then the NOMMO Literary Society has lost most of its materials in the tragedy. However, Salaam continues to teach writing and video production to high school students in New Orleans public schools and with Students at the Center. Salaam has coined the term "Neo-Griot" to describe his method of working with "text, sound, and light" to help a new generation of writers tell their stories using video technology.

11 The Community Book Center reopened after Hurricane Katrina in December 2006.

12 Dr. Wade Nobles is a psychologist and the Director of Black Studies at California State University, San Francisco.

5 Catching the Fire

1 Banneker noted this quote came from Jomo Kenyatta.
2 The Schomburg Center for Research in Black Culture is a part of the New York City Public Library system. The Schomburg is committed to preserving the histories of people throughout the African Diaspora.
3 Sonia Sanchez participated on a panel that revisited the contributions of the Black Arts Movement at Emory University on Wednesday, October 17, 2007.

Bibliography

Adoff, A., & Brooks, G. (1973). *The poetry of Black America: Anthology of the 20th Century.* New York: HarperCollins.

African American Students Association. (December 1, 1969). "The 15 demands of the African-American Students' Association." *Black News,* 1(5), 6.

African Free School has own methodology. (June 26, 1971). *New York Amsterdam News,* pp. D-2.

Alexander, E. (Ed.). (2005). *The essential Gwendolyn Brooks.* American Poets Project: The Library of America.

Alim, H. S. (2005). Critical language awareness in the United States: Revisiting issues and revising pedagogies in a resegregated society. *Educational Researcher,* 34 (7), 24–31.

Alim, H. S. & Baugh, J. (Eds.) (2006). *Talking Black talk: Language, education, and social change.* New York: Teachers College Press.

Anderson, J. (1988). *The education of Blacks in the South, 1860–1935.* Chapel Hill, NC: UNC Press.

Anderson, E. (1992). *Streetwise: Race, class and change in an urban community.* Chicago: University of Chicago.

Anderson, E. (2000). *Code of the street: Decency, violence and the moral life of the inner city.* New York: Norton.

Anderson, E. (2003). *A place on the corner* (2nd ed.) Chicago: University of Chicago.

Apple, M. (2004). *Ideology and curriculum.* New York: RoutledgeFalmer.

Austin, A. (2006) *Achieving Blackness: Race, Black nationalism, and Afrocentrism in the twentieth century.* New York and London: New York University Press.

Baker, H. A. (1988). *Afro American poetics: Revisions of Harlem and the Black aesthetic.* Chicago: University of Chicago Press.

Baldwin, J. (1963). *The fire next time.* New York: Vintage Books.

Ball, A. F. (1995). Text design patterns in the writing of urban African American students: Teaching to the cultural strengths of students in multicultural settings. *Urban Education,* 30(3), 253–289.

Ball, A. F. & Lardner, T. (2005). *African American literacies unleashed: Vernacular English in the composition classroom.* Carbondale,, IL: Southern Illinois University Press.

Bandele, A. (May 2003). "The life of an outlaw." *VIBE,* 136–138.

Baraka, A. (1995). "SOS." In W.J. Harris (Ed.), *The LeRoi Jones/Amiri Baraka Reader* (p. 218). New York: Thunder's Mouth Press.

Baugh. J. (1983). *Black street speech: Its history, structure, and survival.* Austin, TX: University of Texas Press.

Berhan, S. (October 1969). "Explanation of the so-called generation gap." *Black News,* 1(1), 2.

Black and Allied Students Association of New York University. (August/September 1971). The East: A Model of Nationhood. *Imani,* 5, 28–39.

Black Books Bulletin interviews Gwen Brooks. (1974) *Black Books Bulletin,* 2(1), 28–35.

Black children . . . the world is yours. (February 15, 1970). *Black News,* 1(9), 8.

Black Nation Education Series #7. (1970). *Outline for New African Educational Institution: The Uhuru Sasa Program.* Brooklyn, New York: The EAST

Black News of Bedford Stuyvesant. (October, 1969). *Black News,* 1(1), 1.

Black Study Circle. (October, 1969). *Black News,* 1(1), 3.

Black Study Circle. (November 15, 1969). *Black News,* 1(4), 3.

Black Theatre. (September 26, 1970). *Black News,* 1(21), 15.

Black United Fund of Sacramento Valley Inc. African American Nonprofit Leadership. (Fall/Winter 2006–2007). "The Sacramento Kwanzaa Story, Past & Present." 1, 2: 1–2.

Bolden, B.J. (1999). *Urban Rage in Bronzeville: Social commentary in the poetry of Gwendolyn Brooks, 1945–1960.* Chicago: Third World Press.

Boyd, M. J. (2003). *Wrestling with the muse: Dudley Randall and the Broadside Press.* New York: Columbia University Press

Brooks, G. (1945). *A street in Bronzeville.* (3rd ed.) New York: Harper & Row.

Brooks, G. (1964). *In the Mecca.* New York: Harper & Row.

Brooks, G. (1970). *Family pictures.* Detroit, MI: Broadside Press.

Brooks, G. (1971). *Jump Bad: A new Chicago anthology.* Detroit, MI: Broadside Press.

Brooks, G. (1972). *Report from part one.* Detroit, MI: Broadside Press.

Brooks, G. (1975a). Prologue. The new preparation. Aims. Subject matter. Method. The hard flower. In G., Brooks, K., Kgositsile, H. R.,

Brooks, G. (Fall 1975b). Of flowers and fire and flowers. *Black Books Bulletin,* 3(2), 16–18.

Brooks, G. (1996). *Report from part two.* Chicago: Third World Press.

Brooks, G., & Alexander, E. (2005). *The essential Gwendolyn Brooks.* Library of America.

Brooks, G., Kgositsile, K., Madhubuti, H. R., & Randall, D. (1975). *A capsule course in Black poetry writing.* Detroit, MI: Broadside Press.

Brown, F. P. (1999). *Performing the word: African American poetry as vernacular culture.* New Brunswick, NJ: Rutgers University Press.

Brown, S. (2003). *Fighting for US: Malauna Karenga, the US organization and Black Cultural Nationalism.* New York: New York University Press.

Buras, K. L. (forthcoming). Reconstruction, race, and resistance in New Orleans: Can a city school the nation? New York: Routledge.

Buras, K. & Apple, M. (2006). The subaltern speak: Curriculum, power, and educational struggles. In M. Apple & K. Buras (Eds.) *The subaltern speak: Curriculum, power, and educational struggles* (pp. 1–39). New York and London: Routledge.

Campbell, L. (October 1969). Ocean Hill-Brownsville revisited: 1969. *Black News,* 1(2), 1–3.

Campbell, L. (December 19, 1969). In search of the new world. *Black News,* 1(6), 4–5.

Campbell, L./Big Black. (July 6, 1970). Around our way. *Black News,* 1(17), 4.

Césaire, A. (1969). *A season in the Congo.* New York: Grove Press.

Christmas Nigger. (November 15, 1969). *Black News,* 1(4), 1.

Churchville, J. V. (January 25, 1970). On Correct Black Education. *Black News,* 1(8), 1–3.

Clarke, C. (2006). *"After Mecca": Women poets and the Black Arts Movement.* New Brunswick, NJ: Rutgers University Press.

Collins, L.G., & Crawford, M. N. (2006). Introduction: Power to the People! The art of Black Power. In L.G. Collins & M. N. Crawford (Eds.), *New thoughts on the Black Arts Movement* (pp. 1–19). New Brunswick, NJ: Rutgers University Press.

Cook-Gumperz, J. (2006). "Literacy and schooling: an unchanging equation?" In J. Cook-Gumperz (Ed.), *The Social Construction of Literacy* Second Edition (pp. 19–49). Cambridge: Cambridge University Press.

Crawford, M. N. (2006). Black light on the Wall of Respect: The Chicago Black Arts Movement. In L.G. Collins and M. N. Crawford (Eds.), *New thoughts on the Black Arts Movement* (pp. 23–42). New Brunswick, NJ: Rutgers University Press.

Datcher, M. (2001). *Raising fences: A black man's love story.* New York: Riverhead Books.

Davis, M. (1959/1997). *Kind of Blue.* [CD]. Sony Music.

Delpit, L. (1995). *Other people's children: Cultural conflict in the classroom.* New York: New Press.

Douglass, F. (1968). *The narrative of the life of Frederick Douglass: An American slave.* New York: Signet.

Duneier, M. (2000). *Sidewalk.* New York: Farrar, Strauss, & Giroux.

Fanon, F. (1963/2005). *The wretched of the earth.* New York: Grove Press.

Fisher, M. (2003a). Choosing Literacy: African Diaspora Participatory Literacy Communities. Unpublished dissertation: University of California, Berkeley.

Fisher, M. (2003b). Open mics and open minds: Spoken word poetry in African Diaspora Participatory Literacy Communities. *Harvard Educational Review,* 73 (3), 362–389.

Fisher, M. T. (2004). "The song is unfinished": The new literate and the literary and their institutions. *Written Communication,* 21 (3): 290–312.

Fisher, M.T. (January 2005a). Literocracy: Liberating language and creating possibilities. *English Education,* 37 (2): 92–95.

Fisher, M. T. (January 2005b). From the coffee house to the school house: The promise and potential of spoken word poetry in school contexts. *English Education,* 37(2): 115–131.

Fisher, M. T. (March 2006a). Earning "dual degrees": Black bookstores as alternative knowledge spaces. *Anthropology and Education Quarterly,* 37(1): 83–99.

Fisher, M. T. (2006b). Building a literocracy: Diaspora literacy and heritage knowledge in Participatory Literacy Communities. In A. Ball (Ed.), *With more deliberate speed: Achieving equity and excellence in education—Realizing the full potential of Brown v. Board of Education.* National Society for the Study of Education.

Fisher, M. T. (2007a). *Writing in Rhythm: Spoken word poetry in urban classrooms.* New York: Teachers College Press.

Fisher, M. T. (2007b). "Every city has soldiers": The role of intergenerational relationships in Participatory Literacy Communities. *Research in the Teaching of English,* 37(2) 139–162.

Foner, P. S. (1950). *The life and writings of Frederick Douglass, the early years.* New York: International Publishers.

Forman, R. (1993). *We are the young magicians.* Boston: Beacon Press.

Foundation for Change in NYC. Fact sheets on institutional racism.

Franklin, V.P. (1994). *Black self-determination: A cultural history of African-American resistance.* Chicago: Lawrence Hill.

Freire, P. (2003). *Pedagogy of the oppressed. (30th Anniversary Edition).* New York and London: Continuum International Publishing Group Inc.

Freire, P. & Macedo, D. (1987). *Literacy: Reading the word and the world.* Westport, CT: Bergin & Garvey.

Fuller, Hoyt, Interview. (1971). *Black Books Bulletin.* Chicago: Institute of Positive Education.

Gates, H. L. & McKay, N.Y. (Eds.). (1997). *Norton anthology of African-American literature.* New York: Norton.

Gavin, C., Alford, L., Williams, V., & Mair, A. (2000). "They schools" [Recorded by Dead Prez]. On *Let's get free* [CD]. New York: Loud Records.

Gayles, G. W. (Ed.) (2003). *Conversations with Gwendolyn Brooks.* Jackson: The University Press of Mississippi.

Gilbert, D. I. M. (1998). *Catch the fire: A cross-generational anthology of contemporary African American poetry.* New York: Riverhead Books.

Gilbert, J. (November 15, 1969). From sisters to sisters. *Black News,* 1(4), 8.

Gilbert, J. (December 1, 1969). The soap opera syndrome. *Black News,* 1(5), 3.

Gilbert, J. (January 10, 1970). The games black folks play. *Black News,* 1(7), 4–5.

Giovanni, N. (1970). *Black feeling, Black talk, Black judgment.* New York: William Morrow Publishers.

Gonzalez, N., Moll, L. & Amanti, C. (2005). *Funds of knowledge: Theorizing practice in households, communities and classrooms.* Mahwah, NJ: Lawrence Erlbaum Associates, Inc.

Gordon, J. A. (2001). *Why they couldn't wait: A critique of the Black-Jewish conflict over community control in Ocean Hill—Brownsville (1967–1971).* New York and London: RoutledgeFalmer.

Gorman, B. (1971). New school aims to aid black youth. *The Sacramento Observer.*

Graff, H. (2001). The nineteenth century origins of our times. In E. Cushman, E. R. Kintgen, B.M. Kroll, & M. Rose (Eds.), *Literacy: A critical sourcebook* (pp. 211–233). New York: St Martin's.

Gutman, H. (1987). Schools for Freedom: The post-emancipation origins of Afro-American education. In I. Berlin (Ed.), *Power & Culture: Essays on the American working class* (pp. 260–297). New York: Pantheon Books.

Hale, T. A. (1998). *Griots and griottes: Masters of words and music.* Bloomington and Indianapolis: Indiana University Press.

Harding, V. (1990). *Hope and history: Why we must share the story of the movement.* Maryknoll, New York: Orbis Books.

Hay, S. A. (2003). *African American theatre: An historical and critical analysis.* Cambridge: Cambridge University Press.

Heath, S.B. (1981). Towards an ethnohistory of writing in American education. In M. Whiteman (Ed.), *Variation in writing: Functional and linguistic-cultural differences.* (pp. 25–45). Hillsdale, NJ: Lawrence Erlbaum Associates.

Heath, S. B. (1983). *Ways with words: Language, life, and work in communities and classrooms.* Cambridge: Cambridge University Press.

Hill, L. (1998). *The miseducation of Lauryn Hill.* [CD] New York: Ruffhouse Records.

Holt, T. (1990). "'Knowledge is power': The Black struggle for literacy" (pp. 91–102). In A. A. Lunsford, H. Moglen, & J. Slevin (Eds.), *The right to literacy.* New York: The Modern Language Association of America.

Irvine, J. J. (2002). *In search of wholeness: African American teachers and their culturally specific classroom practices.* New York: Palgrave Macmillan.

Irvine, J. J. (2003). *Educating teachers for diversity: Seeing with a cultural eye.* New York: Teachers College Press.

Jahn, J. (1961). *Muntu: African culture and the western world.* New York: Grove Press.

Jones, L. (1971). The changing same (R&B and new black music). In A. Gayle (Ed.), *The black aesthetic* (pp. 118–131). New York: Doubleday and Company, Inc.

Jones, L., & Neal, L. (1969). *Black fire.* New York: William Morrow Publishers.

Joseph, P. E. (Ed.) (2006a). *The Black Power Movement: Rethinking the Civil Rights—Black Power era.* New York and London: Routledge.

Joseph, P. E. (2006b). *Waiting 'til the midnight hour.* New York: Henry, Holt & Co.

Kelley, R. D. G. (2002). *Freedom dreams: The Black radical imagination.* Boston: Beacon Press.

King, J. E. (2006). "If justice is our objective"—Diaspora literacy, heritage knowledge and the praxis of critical studyin' for human freedom. In A. Ball (Ed.), *With more deliberate speed: Achieving equity and excellence in education.* National Society for the Study of Education Yearbook. Malden, MS: Blackwell Publishing.

King, M. L. (1986). The trumpet of consciousness. In J. M. Washington (Ed.), *A testament of hope: The essential writings of Martin Luther King Jr.* San Francisco: Harper & Row Publishers.

King, W. (February 19, 1973). Urban school problems intensify in Philadelphia. *New York Times,* p. 1.

Kinloch, V. (2006). *June Jordan: Her life and letters.* Westport, CT: Praeger.

Knight, E. (1968). *Poems from prison.* Detroit: Broadside Press.

Konadu, K. (2005). *Truth crushed to the earth will rise again: The EAST organization and the principles and practice of Black Nationalist development.* Trenton, NJ and Asmara, Eritrea: African World Press.

Kweli, T. (1999). "K.O.S. (Determination)." [Recorded by Black Star]. On *Mos Def & Talib Kweli are Black Star.* [CD]. New York: Rawkus Records.

Ladson-Billings, G. (1997). *The dreamkeepers: Successful teachers of African American children.* San Francisco: Jossey-Bass.

Ladson-Billings, G. (2001). *Crossing over to Canaan: The journey of new teachers in diverse classrooms.* San Francisco: Jossey-Bass.

Ladson-Billings, G. (2005). Reading, writing, and race: Literacy practices of teachers in diverse classrooms. In T. McCarty (Ed.), *Language, literacy, and power in schooling.* (pp. 133–150). Maweh, NJ: Lawrence Erlbaum Associates, Publishers.

Lee, C. D. (1992). Profile of an Independent Black Institution: African-centered education at work. *Journal of Negro Education,* 61(2), 160–177.

Lee, C. D. (1995). A culturally based cognitive apprenticeship: Teaching African American high school students skills in literary interpretation. *Reading Research Quarterly,* 30(4): 608–629.

Lee, C.D. (2006). "Every goodbye ain't gone: Analyzing the cultural underpinnings of classroom talk." *International Journal of Qualitative Studies in Education,* 19(3), 305–327.

Lee, C. D. (2007). *Culture, literacy, and learning: Taking bloom in the midst of the whirlwind.* New York: Teachers College Press.

Lee, D. L. (1971a). Toward a Definition: Black poetry of the sixties (After LeRoi Jones). In A. Gayle (Ed.), *The black aesthetic* (pp. 235–247). Garden City, New York: Doubleday & Company, Inc.

Lee, D. L. (1971b). What we're about. *Black Books Bulletin.* Chicago: Institute of Positive Education.

Lee, D. L. (1972). Preface: Gwendolyn Brooks: Beyond the wordmaker—The making of an African poet. In G. Brooks, *Report from part one.* Detroit: Broadside Press.

Liles, G. (2000). *On the road to Damascus.* New York: Division of Words.

Madhubuti, & D. Randall, (Eds.), *A capsule course in Black poetry writing.* Detroit, MI: Broadside Press.

Madhubuti, H. R. (1973). *From plan to planet: Life-Studies: The need for Afrikan minds and institutions.* Chicago: Third World Press.

Madhubuti, S. N. (1974). Focus on form in Gwendolyn Brooks. *Black Books Bulletin,* 2(1), 25–27.

Marable, M. (2006). *Living black history: How reimagining the African-American past can remake America's racial future.* New York: Basic Civitas Books.

Martin, T. (1983). *Literary Garveyism: Garvey, Black Arts and the Harlem Renaissance.* Dover, MA: Majority Press.

Matsuoka, B. M. (Executive Producer). (2003). *The expanding canon: Critical pedagogy with Abiodun Oyewole and Lawson Fusau Inada* [Television Broadcast]. New York: Thirteen/WNET.

Mayes, K. (2006). "A Holiday of Our Own": Kwanzaa, cultural nationalism, and the promotion of a Black Power holiday, 1966–1985. In P. Joseph (Ed.), *The Black Power Movement: Rethinking the Civil Rights–Black Power era* (pp. 229–249). New York and London: Routledge.

McHenry, E. (2002). *Forgotten readers: Recovering the lost history of African American literary societies.* Durham, NC: Duke University Press.

McHenry, E., & Heath, S. B. (1994). The literate and the literary: African Americans as writers and readers–1830–1940. *Written Communication,* 11(4), 419–443.

McMillan, T. (1992). *Waiting to exhale.* New York: Viking.

Melhem, D. H. (1990). "Gwendolyn Brooks: Humanism and heroism" (pp. 11–38). In D.H. Melhem (Ed.), *Heroism in the new black poetry: Introductions and interviews.* Lexington, KY: University of Kentucky Press.

Mendes. (1971). *African heritage cookbook.* New York: Macmillan Publishing Company.

Moll, L., & Gonzalez, N. (2001). Lessons from research with language-minority children (pp. 156–171). In E. Cushman, E. R. Kintgen, B. M. Kroll, & M. Rose (Eds.), *Literacy: A critical sourcebook.* Boston: St. Martin's Press.

Morris, R. C. (1981). *Reading, 'riting, and reconstruction: The education of freedman in the South 1861–1870.* Chicago and London: The University of Chicago Press.

Mullen, B. V. (1999). Engendering the cultural front: Gwendolyn Brooks, Black women, and class struggle in poetry. In B. V. Mullen (Ed.), *Popular fronts: Chicago and African-American cultural politics, 1935–1946* (pp. 149–180). Urbana and Chicago: University of Illinois Press.

Muller, L. (Ed.). (1995). *Poetry for the people: A revolutionary blueprint.* New York: Routledge.

Neal, L. (1971). The Black Arts Movement. In A. Gayle (Ed.), *The black aesthetic* (pp. 272–290). Garden City, New York: Double Day & Company Inc.

New breed of Black youth. (December 10, 1970). *Black News,* 1(25), 1–4.

Nyerere, J. K. (1968). *Ujamaa: Essays on socialism.* Nairobi: Oxford University Press.

Odinga, O. (1969). *Not yet uhuru: An autobiography.* New York: Hill & Wang.

Olson, D. (2001). Writing and the mind. In E. Cushman, E. R. Kintgen, B.M. Kroll, & M. Rose (Eds.), *Literacy: A critical sourcebook* (pp. 107–122). New York: St. Martin's.

Our young bloods at "Our Lady of Victory" (March 21, 1970). *Black News,* 1(11), 5.

Ong, W. J., S.J. (2001). Writing is a technology that restructures thought. In E. Cushman, E. R. Kintgen, B.M. Kroll, & M. Rose (Eds.) *Literacy: A critical sourcebook* (pp. 19–31). New York: St. Martin's.

Organized Noize, Bell, F., Gipp, C., & Patton, A. (1995). "Dirty South" [Recorded by Goodie Mob]. On *Soul Food* [CD]. New York: LaFace Records.

Parents Association of P.S. 305. (March 21, 1970). Message to parents. *Black News,* 1(11), 4.

Perry, T. (2003). Freedom for literacy and literacy for freedom: The African American philosophy of education. In T. Perry, C. Steele, & A. Hilliard (Eds.), *Young, gifted, and Black: Promoting high achievement among African-American students* (pp. 11–51). Boston: Beacon Press.

Peterson, C. L. (1995). *"Doers of the Word": African-American women speakers & writers in the North (1830–1880)*. Oxford and New York: Oxford University Press.

Podair, J. E. (2002). *The strike that changed New York: Blacks, whites, and the Ocean Hill-Brownsville Crisis.* New Haven, CT: Yale University Press.

Pritchett, W. (2002). *Brownsville, Brooklyn: Blacks, Jews, and the changing face of the ghetto.* Chicago: The University of Chicago Press.

Richardson, E. (2006). *Hip hop literacies.* New York: Routledge.

Rickford, J.R., & Rickford, R.J. (2000). *Spoken Soul: The story of Black English.* New York: John Wiley & Sons, Inc.

Roach, M. (1960/1988). *We insist! Max Roach's freedom now suite.* [CD]. New York: Candid Records.

Salaam, K., & Alexander, K. (1998). *360 degrees: A revolution of black poets.* New Orleans: Black Words in association with Runagate Press.

Sanchez, S. (1970). *Liberation poem.* Detroit: Broadside Press.

Saul, S. (2005). *Freedom is, Freedom ain't: Jazz and the making of the sixties.* Cambridge, MA: Harvard University Press.

Saunders, R. (March 28, 1971). Amiri Baraka at Kimako's. *Black News,* 1(30), 22.

Scribner, S. & Cole, M. (1981). Unpackaging literacy. In M. Farr Whiteman (Ed.), *Writing: The nature, development and teaching of written communication* (pp. 71–87). Mahwah, NJ: Lawrence Erlbaum Associates.

Shakur, A. (1987). *Assata: An autobiography.* Chicago: Lawrence Hill Books.

Shor, I. (1992). *Empowering education: Critical teaching for social change.* Chicago: University of Chicago Press.

Siddle Walker, V. (1996). *Their highest potential: An African American school community in the segregated south.* Durham, NC: University of North Carolina Press.

Simpson, L. M. A. (2004). *Images of America: Sacramento's Oak Park.* San Francisco, CA: Arcadia Publishing.

Smart & Grosvenor, V. (1970). *Vibration cooking, or the travel notes of a Geechee Girl.* New York: Doubleday.

Smith, L. (2006). Black Arts to Def Jam: Performing Black "spirit work" across generations. In L. G. Collins and M. N. Crawford (Eds.), *New thoughts on the Black Arts Movement* (pp. 349–367). New Brunswick, NJ: Rutgers University Press.

Smitherman, G. (1999). How I got ovuh: African world view and Afro-American oral tradition. In G. Smitherman (Ed.), *Talkin that talk: Language, culture and education in African America* (pp. 199–222). London & New York: Routledge.

Sonny Carson's education is the way we all learn ultimately. (July 1974). *Black News,* 2, 19, 24.

Street, B. V. (2005). Recent applications of New Literacy Studies in educational contexts. *Research in the Teaching of English,* 39, 4: 417–423.

Sutton, S. (2004) Spoken word: Performance poetry in the Black community. In J. Mahiri (Ed.), *What they don't learn in school: Literacy in the lives of urban youth.* (pp. 213–242). New York: Peter Lang.

Tate, C. (Ed.) (1983). *Black women writers at work.* New York: Continuum.

Thompson, J. E. (1999). *Dudley Randall, Broadside Press, and the Black Arts Movement in Detroit, 1960–1995.* Jefferson, NC: McFarland & Company, Inc. Publishers.

Tobias, R. (December 19, 1969). The Uhuru Academy. *Black News,* 1(6), 3.

Towns, S. (1974). Black autobiography and the dilemma of western artistic traditions. *Black Books Bulletin,* 2(1), 17–23.

Turner, J. (1993). David Walker and the Appeal: An introduction. In D. Walker *David Walker's Appeal to the colored citizens of the world in particular, and very expressly, to those of the United States of America.* Baltimore, MD: Black Classic Press.

Understanding. (November 15, 1969). *Black News,* 1(4), 3.

Walker, D. ([1830] 1993). *David Walker's Appeal to the colored citizens of the world, but in particular, and very expressly, to those of the United States of America.* Baltimore, MD: Black Classic Press.

Walmsley, A. (1992). *The Caribbean Artists Movement, 1966–1972: A literary and cultural history.* London: New Beacon Books.

Weusi, J. (January 10, 1970). Around our way. *Black News,* 1(7), 4.

Weusi, J. (February 15, 1970). Around our way. *Black News,* 1(9), 5.

Weusi, J./Big Black. (March 21, 1970). Around our way. *Black News,* 1(11), 14

Weusi, J./Big Black. (February 25, 1971). Around our way. *Black News*, 1(29), 6–7.

Weusi, J./Big Black. (January 1972). Around our way: 1972—The year of black politics? *Black News*, 1(37), 11–13.

Weusi, J. (March 15, 1973). Around our way. *Black News*, 1 (46), 27–28.

Weusi, J. (January 28, 1974). Around our way. *Black News*, 2(13), 12.

Why your child gets low grades. (April 10, 1970). *Black News*, 1(12), 3.

Wilcox, P. (Ed.). (September 1, 1968). Report from education workshop #1 Control of schools within the Black community. Philadelphia, PA., Third Annual Black Power Conference.

Woodson, C. G. ([1933] 1969). *Mis-education of the Negro*. Washington D.C: The Associated Publishers, Inc.

Wright-Lewis, C. (2001). *Maurya's Seed—Why hope lives behind project walls*. New York: Universe/Writers Club Press.

Index

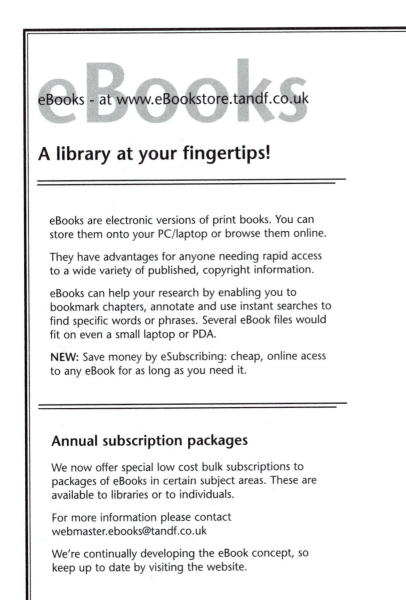